XXᵀᴴ CENTURY
DRAWINGS AND WATERCOLORS

XXᵀᴴ CENTURY
DRAWINGS AND WATERCOLORS

BY
RAYMOND COGNIAT

CROWN PUBLISHERS, INC. · NEW YORK

Translated from the French by
ANNE ROSS

PAUL SIGNAC   St. Michel Mountain   Pencil   Museum of Modern Art, Paris

INTRODUCTION

DRAWING AND WATER-COLOUR AS AUTONOMOUS ART-FORMS

Drawing and water-colour — even in the form of tinted drawings — hold
an important place in the history of painting, though they are often considered minor
arts. In general they allow a painter, before arriving at his definitive work, to experiment, study detail, make preparatory sketches and draft out the main structure
which will determine the whole shape of the final work. Drawing and wash drawings are the means by which a painter becomes acquainted with his subject. In past
centuries drawing was of course often an end in itself: a complete language which
needed no extraneous additions. For instance, Dürer's *Hare* and *Tuft of Grass* are
" complete " works. Rembrandt's drawings are also complete and convey the subtlety of mood and perspective of coloured vistas; Poussin's colour washes and even
Fragonard's sepias give the impression of finality, of work fully achieved and per-

EDOUARD VUILLARD Seated Nude Pencil Museum of Modern Art, Paris

fected. Such examples are relatively rare, and were the forerunners of the modern tendency to elevate studies from their auxiliary rôle to the position of perfect and definitive expressions on a level with oil-paintings.

It was the nineteenth century which seriously championed this attitude. Certain art-collectors had already proved that there was deep pleasure to be gained from the possession and contemplation of drawings, to which still extant collections made by famous connoisseurs bear witness. This taste developed in the eighteenth century and spread to an ever-growing public through the invention of new techniques for engraving in the style of drawings or pastels, which set the course for this fashion. The discovery of lithography accentuated the trend, and this time did not transpose the artist's work but reproduced it direct without any intermediate process.

In the nineteenth century the new copying techniques had increased the circulation of drawings beyond all expectations. Journals had been successfully launched, thanks partly to these new processes, but to make them more interesting and attractive to their ever-growing public, they had to be illustrated. Former plates

7

8

PIERRE BONNARD   Children in the Garden
Pastel   Bühler Collection, Winterthur

ALBERT MARQUET   Seated Woman
Indian Ink   Romanet Gallery, Paris

AUGUSTE RODIN Nude Water Colour and Pencil Former Majovsky Collection, Budapest

PABLO PICASSO   Mother and Child
India Ink and Water Colour   Former Collection Ferenc Hatvany, Budapest

were unsuitable, as they were inserted anywhere between the pages of books and were now useless for the new printing methods. The format of books was completely transformed, because illustrations now appeared as lithographs and were interspersed with the text throughout the book.

Newspapers and reviews contributed to this movement, topical periodicals grew in number and by facilitating travel the invention of the railway gave birth to tourist literature. In addition political polemics found a useful adjunct in the cartoonist, and all these developments which called for the collaboration of artists began to make drawing an end in itself. New possibilities, new incentives and new styles suited to them were discovered, and between caricature and reportage drawing became a vehicle for conveying direct information and no longer just a preparatory study for more definitive work.

By the end of the eighteenth century an excellent artist, Gabriel de Saint Aubin, had foreseen that an artist could play the part of a reporter. His notebooks were full of scribbled sketches and heralded the work of those specialists who in the following century derived their inspiration from news items to meet the demands of informative journals. One of these specialists, Constantin Guys, was even considered by Baudelaire one of the greatest artists of his day.

Gradually, and with an ever-quickening, continuous impulse, the invention and perfection of the processes of mechanical reproduction speeded this development and gave an increasingly independent function to drawing, which became steadily more indispensable to the modern publishing processes. There arose a new group of artists serving these processes with water-colours, gouaches and drawings completely liberated from the old disciplines. They became artist-reporters, humorous artists, commercial artists and in many cases illustrators of books.

Painting as such was of course affected by these changed conditions, but did not immediately react to the new schools of art which since impressionism have been primarily concerned with pictorial forms, i.e. subject, colour, construction, etc. in determining pigmentary texture. Drawing adapted itself in proportion to its subordination to painting.

Even in this seemingly auxiliary rôle drawing preserved an essential function, because it expressed the initial inspiration. More than ever before it has become a spontaneous act, the first expression of a thought, almost a confidence, in which the artist hardly controls his reactions, whereas a painting leaves as little as possible to chance. It is this intimate, appealing and personal aspect of drawing which has interested countless art-collectors, and the sketch, apparently the most negligible of a great artist's work, has taken its place in collections beside the most finished works.

Simultaneously with the development of this taste for spontaneity, many artists turned to water-colour, gouache and drawing to provide them with a definitive and independent means of expression. Far from being spontaneous, they used these art-forms to execute works as deliberate and considered as any of their oil-paintings. The names of Rouault and Dunoyer de Segonzac are sufficient evidence of the success of this approach, and one could easily add many more examples to prove the to-

PAUL SIGNAC   Beside the River
Water Colour   Former Majovsky Collection, Budapest

Janvier 1913

R de la Fresnaye

ROGER DE LA FRESNAYE
Pencil Drawing   Mr. and Mrs. Isadore Levin Collection, Palm Beach, Florida

tal autonomy of these previously auxiliary forms, which now permitted artists to extend the range, variety and flexibility of their vehicles of expression.

LINE-DRAWING

The various kinds of drawing can be grouped under two headings: line-drawing and brush-drawing. Each kind is related to a particular conception and a particular aesthetic, thus proving that they are far removed from the character of oil-painting, which cannot supplement their finished form.

Line-drawing, which emphatically affirms this difference in techniques, carries an abstract and immediately apparent intellectual message. In fact it is possible in a drawing with shadows and perspective to approach a realistic portrayal, to give a sense of space, volume and density by means allied to those of painting, but line-drawing gives no opportunity for subterfuge and only allows one to hint at volume with an outline, at movement with a curve and at space and texture with even more remote and obscure means which depend on the artist's creative ingenuity. How is it that Matisse's drawings are so marvellously evocative without perspective, hatching or shadows? How is it that he can evoke the texture of skin or textile with a line around a face or a cushion? This kind of drawing demands a skill which is the culmination of art and is achieved only by the very great. While looking extremely simple it is in fact the very opposite of a casual sketch; an accomplishment without corollary. The same applies to Dufy's drawings of rural scenes or seascapes, which manage to convey with a paradoxically scientific simplicity not only movement and space, but light, the trembling of foliage and almost even colour. Taken at this level, drawing is as independent a process as oil-painting, but creates its effects through a complete, original transposition of reality. It is a wholly intellectual and symbolic act, like calligraphy or hieroglyphics. The feelings inherent in it have virtually nothing to do with the subject, but with the nature of the lines themselves, so that they become a kind of writing, which one could study with a method similar to that used for graphology.

The same ideas apply equally to another, more spontaneous and less deliberate, form of line-drawing, the most typical example of which to-day is Dunoyer de Segonzac. His works are certainly less controlled or organized than those of Matisse or Dufy; rather he seems anxious to preserve the appearance of improvization and of direct sensation, so that his art is in fact related to the impressionist school, through ideas if not through technique. As though wanting to stress this affinity his most frequent subjects are landscapes, with all that this choice requires in terms of instinctive ability to convey the fluidity of form, light and atmosphere. In this technique Segonzac joins Corot and like him succeeds in producing a finished work while apparently executing a casual sketch.

Matisse and Dufy consciously strive to create a style; Segonzac has no such wish and yet finds one suited to himself. All these characteristics are to be found in many of the other artists discussed later in this book, and these three have been quoted as examples not because they are preeminent in their field, but because they happen to give the clearest illustration of the points at issue.

In order to appreciate the level of perfection which this draughtsmanship has

ALBERT MARQUET Mirrored Nude Indian Ink Romanet Gallery, Paris

OTHON FRIESZ   Portrait of Fernand Fleuret   Water Colour   Museum of Modern Art, Paris

PABLO PICASSO   Roosters
Water Colour   Cone Collection, Museum of Art, Baltimore

PABLO PICASSO   Family of Acrobats with Monkey ▷
Gouache   Art Museum, Goeteborg, Sweden

HIPPOLYTE PETITJEAN   Ophélie Bresdin
Water Colour   Private Collection

20

Henri Manguin   Oriental Woman   Water Colour   Private Collection, Geneva

21

HENRI EDMOND CROSS Landscape at Lavandou Water Colour Private Collection, Paris

PIERRE BONNARD   Sunset on the Mediterranean   Gouache   Private Collection

HENRI MANGUIN Tulips
Water Colour and Pencil Bühler Collection, Winterthur

JEAN CHARLEMAGNE LAUNOIS Algerian Girls on the Balcony
Water Colour Museum of Modern Art, Paris

25

THÉOPHILE STEINLEN   Nude with a Handkerchief   Pastel   Oscar Ghez Collection, Geneva

SUZANNE VALADON After the Bath
Pastel Private Collection

27

JULIUS PASCIN   Seated Model
Pastel and Coloured Crayon   Romanet Gallery, Paris

28

MAXIMILIEN LUCE   Woman Laundering
Gouache   Private Collection

reached, it is helpful to recall that in Renaissance treatises on perspective, line-drawing is used to illustrate the effect of vanishing lines in the suggestion of space, thereby stressing the value of almost abstract transcription above that of sensuous treatment. This almost implies reducing the technique to its mechanical effects and limiting its use to geometrical delineation of space. However the work of all the painters just mentioned contains an emphasis on sensitivity and a modified freedom beyond the reach of formulas, because the individual approach here matters more than an applied set of rules. That which started as a technical exercise, or in the case of the earlier artists a material necessity due to the shortage of means of expression, has become the contrary, and in modern art is an end in itself of unfathomed potentiality.

One must acknowledge the considerable contribution of late nineteenth century Japanese and Chinese artists to enriching and vitalizing line-drawing. Vincent Van Gogh, above all, came deeply under their influence and his line-drawings are among the most powerful examples of the genre.

ROGER DE LA FRESNAYE Landscape with Nude
Indian Ink Private Collection, Paris

JUAN GRIS Man with Glass Pencil Louise Leiris Gallery, Paris

BRUSH-DRAWING

Brush-drawing seems more closely allied to oil-painting, and does in fact often merge with water-colouring. Colour-washing is indeed drawing with a brush, but is also water-colour, both technically and in the finished effect. Subordination to painting itself has been also eliminated here and brush-drawing is in most cases no longer used only for detail study and preparation for a definitive work. Most twentieth-century water-colours and brush-drawings are independent works which stand on their own, and in the nineteenth century this trend was already clearly affirmed, but

31

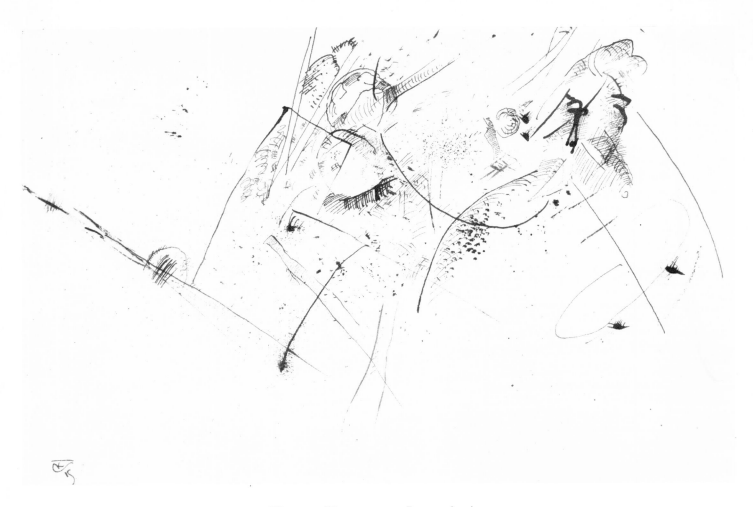

WASSILY KANDINSKY Improvisation
Pen and Ink Mr. and Mrs. Isadore Levin Collection, Palm Beach, Florida

even Delacroix's works of this genre are more often preparatory studies. With the coming of impressionism and the fashion for seizing nature in her most fleeting aspects, with the attendant necessity for working rapidly in order to preserve unchanged the original sensation, water-colours and colour-washes became independent, original works.

From Jongkind to Signac there grew a desire to use the whiteness of paper and the transparency of colour to obtain effects, especially a lightness of contrast, which painting with oil cannot give, and which better expresses a fluid atmosphere. The great twentieth-century revolutionary movement in art has found a ready-made, highly polished vehicle for its experiments.

If one considers gouache as a very opaque type of water-painting, as easy to execute as a water-colour itself, one realizes how sorely modern artists may have been tempted to find in these techniques an escape-route from the rather too rigid disciplines of oil-painting.

The history of art in the first twenty years of this century provides countless examples of this awareness, this desire for a new departure which is no denial of the past but a leaping of its self-imposed boundaries. As in the previous chapter, two examples can be used to illustrate the nature of this art-form — Rouault and Chagall.

PABLO PICASSO   Woman Standing
Pen and Ink   Mr. and Mrs. Isadore Levin Collection, Palm Beach, Florida

33

The very coupling of these two names shows that there exists no narrow specification in subject or approach, because Rouault's Indian ink drawings convey dramatic intensity of passion, and those of Chagall the gentle lyricism of tender fantasy. While even the lightest of Rouault's gouaches or water-colours are dramatic, Chagall's are ethereal. In both cases one senses none of the tension or effort inherent in oil-painting, but rather a spirit of freedom and independence, in which the senses, rather than arbitrary considerations of form, guide the artist's hand. On this level of expertise and self-reliance colour-washes, water-colours and gouaches can be as definitive as any oil-paintings. Even when water-colour keeps its transparency — as with Segonzac — it is still as concentrated and dense as a canvas. Besides, the artists mentioned are not afraid of grandiose conceptions, because they know how to adjust their medium to their aims.

Though one is tempted to study the artist himself in his line-drawing, by graphological formulas, as though it were his hand-writing, one can attribute no such intellectual content to brush-drawing, which is always more material, more physical, and more allied to a gesture. It is an expression of sensuousness to almost the same extent as oil-painting.

Perhaps the greater popularity of water-colours and colour-washes among contemporary artists exemplifies the increased speed at which we live. Certainly these art-forms allow of no hesitation or alteration. A stroke, once applied, cannot be erased, and even when painted over it is always visible. Self-assurance is therefore a pre-requisite for the artist, since his work will inevitably retain the stamp of his initial sensation and a feeling of improvization. The fact that a taste for spontaneity has developed in both public and artists simultaneously with the increased speed of daily life must be a significant coincidence. The railway, the telephone, then motor transport and the aeroplane have made their mark on all our actions and reactions. Works of art which result from dedicated, deliberate labour cannot satisfy this new desire for speed. A hasty sketch and the spontaneous colour record of water-painting correspond more closely to this idea of the tentative, even the unfinished, which predom-

ARISTIDE MAILLOL   Nude Stretched Out
Sanguine   Private Collection, Paris

inates in most of our actions to-day. There is a pulsing life and nervousness to be felt in the sweep of transparent colour applied to white paper by Rouault or Chagall, as one traces the light and heavy pressure of the artist's hand, suggesting volume and movement without pausing to fill in the details.

The great triumph of our day is to have preserved the provisional aspect of this spontaneous act while giving it — in its most successful instances — a sufficiently decisive, complete character for it to rate as definitive, not needing interpretation or supplement.

GEORGES BRAQUE Study for « The Chair »
Charcoal on Paper Museum of Modern Art, New York

ROGER DE LA FRESNAYE Study
Water Colour Romanet Gallery, Paris

37

Louis Valtat   The Red Dress
Gouache   Romanet Gallery, Paris

André Derain   Two Women
Water Colour   Private Collection ▷

KEES VAN DONGEN Baccarat
Water Colour Museum of Modern Art, Paris

ANDRÉ DERAIN   The Dancers   Water Colour   Private Collection, Paris

41

AMEDEO MODIGLIANI Young Woman with Scarf
Pencil Romanet Gallery, Paris

AMEDEO MODIGLIANI Portrait of a Man
Pencil Romanet Gallery, Paris

ANDRÉ LHOTE
Standing Nude
Sanguine
Private Collection

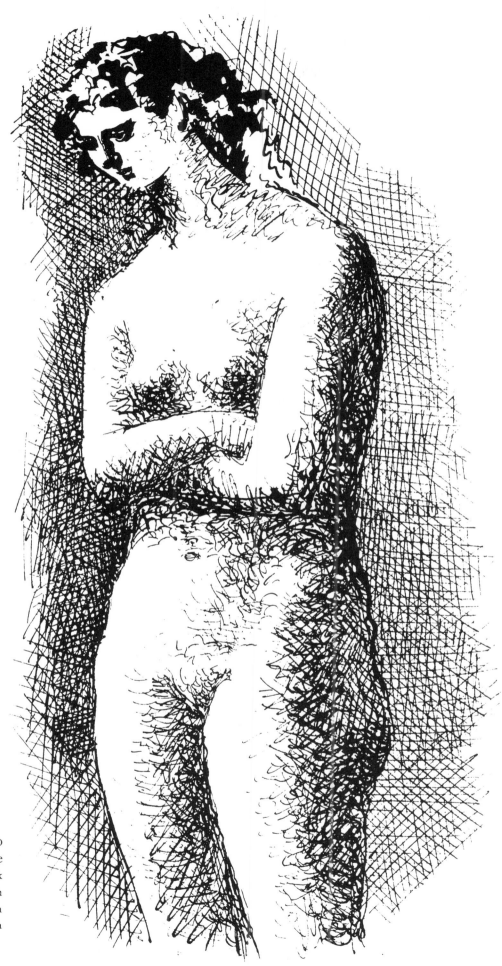

PABLO PICASSO
Standing Nude
Pen and Ink
Mr. and Mrs. Isadore Levin
Collection
Palm Beach, Florida

MAJOR TRENDS

A GENERAL SURVEY

There are certainly no grounds for separating the history of drawing and water-colour entirely from that of oil-painting, and obviously they are closely interdependent, but it is interesting to observe to what extent one reacts on or deviates from the other — in fact to what extent each of these techniques involve differing modes of expression.

A treatise on this one modern artistic trend should begin around the year 1900, because historians agree more and more that in all countries belonging to our western civilization that period saw the start of the major movements which revolutionized the ideas and standpoints on which all art had been based since the Renaissance. The victory of impressionism opened the doors to every kind of daring innovation, and incited artists to abandon slavish adherence to pseudo-tradition. Great movements were born, grew and clashed with increasing rapidity, forcing every artist to study and assess his problems, to take sides, to seek stability and cling to a " master " — a situation which favoured the stronger spirits but threw the others into a sometimes unbearable state of tension. Perhaps as a result more individuality and naturalness emerged in drawing than in painting, for in drawing the artist is more relaxed and less constrained by the desire to assert his personality.

The need for individualism and yet for allegiance to one or other of the major schools is for many painters a serious but involuntary preoccupation, which leads them to strike attitudes and to assert and proclaim their own ideas or those of others beyond their own true resources. A picture is indeed a confession, but a public one, which in the main shows the artist at his own valuation. Drawing, on the other hand, is an intimate daily exercise, like a snapshot or a scribbled memorandum. Its interest for the artist is to escape from that conscious intellectual control and to preserve the immediacy of a feeling in a definitive picture. Even if a drawing is made in a less free, more deliberate mood than that of a simple " note ", it still retains the character of an improvization.

An artist needs this relaxation in which he does not try to judge himself or excel himself, but rather releases his tensions in the interests of self-knowledge. Thus involuntarily, and particularly because it *is* involuntary, he uses a more personal language than when he is conforming to the disciplines of a school or a group. The result is the paradoxical situation of countless modern painters producing drawings and water-colours of greatly superior quality and appeal, because they reflect a genuine sensitivity interpreted by good technique, compared with their oil-paintings, in which they try to apply formulas which do not suit them in order to attain a level they believe to be higher. The unconscious, modest originality of their drawings is much more attractive and authentic than the forced originality of their oil-paintings.

ALBERT LÉON GLEIZES Maternity
Pen and Ink Mr. and Mrs. Isadore Levin Collection, Palm Beach, Florida ▷

FREE TECHNIQUES AT THE END OF THE NINETEENTH AND BEGINNING OF THE TWENTIETH CENTURIES

The Nabis and the Fauves

The end of the nineteenth and the first years of the twentieth centuries were marked by the influence of Japanese art, which grew and spread over a period of several years. Around 1888-1890 it was apparent in some of Gauguin's and Van Gogh's paintings, but was even more evident in the gouaches, water-colours and drawings of younger artists, especially the Nabis, of which Bonnard and Vuillard are the most brilliant representatives. This influence is more apparent in the case of these later artists, because their techniques were closer to the Japanese prints which were their models. A vivid, apparently improvized drawing, embracing the largest possible aspect of life though compressed into a few extremely simplified strokes (a technique mastered centuries ago by artists of the Far East) naturally attracted young devotees of impressionism, with its urge to crystallize a moment of every-day life, though they still longed to break away from their elders and from playing with light and shade, in order to absorb all human life into their art.

The era of the artist's indifference to humanity is past, and the landscape painter seens now too estranged from mankind. Young artists of every school could no longer disregard contemporary social upheavals nor isolate themselves from human problems under the pretext of serving their art. Whether or not they welcome him, man is there in his physical shape and his every-day existence, and the water-colours, gouaches, drawings, pastels and coloured lithographs painted by Bonnard and Vuillard at that time bear witness to this fact, whether they were aware of it or not. Their street-scenes and interiors with human figures or animals caught in some familiar action are all akin to Japanese art, and even some artists who were later to belong to the Fauvist movement followed the same path. Marquet's drawings in particular are strikingly full of analogy and distinguished by vitality and non-malicious irony. They reveal all the characteristics of this artist, whose works could easily feature in an anthology of oriental art.

The best-known and least-disputed example is of course Toulouse-Lautrec. He did not stand alone, but with immense power and persuasive force joined the Nabis (though in a different style) in a movement firmly enough grounded for subsequent artists to go beyond mere imitation. While admitting their allegiance, these followers of the Nabis have succeeded in preserving their identities and in creating a highly representative specimen of western sensibility, rather than a pastiche of Japanese art.

Following in the steps of Toulouse-Lautrec, rather than of the Nabis, other painters have even more emphatically demonstrated their concern with social problems, their partialities or their irony, and seem more committed to emotional illustration of the contemporary scene than to the influence of the exotic. Steinlein,

AMEDEO MODIGLIANI   Study for the « Cariatyd »
Water Colour and Pencil   Museum of Modern Art, Paris

50 MARIE LAURENCIN Portrait of a Young Woman Pastel Museum of Modern Art, Paris

KEES VAN DONGEN   Head of a Woman   Water Colour   Private Collection   51

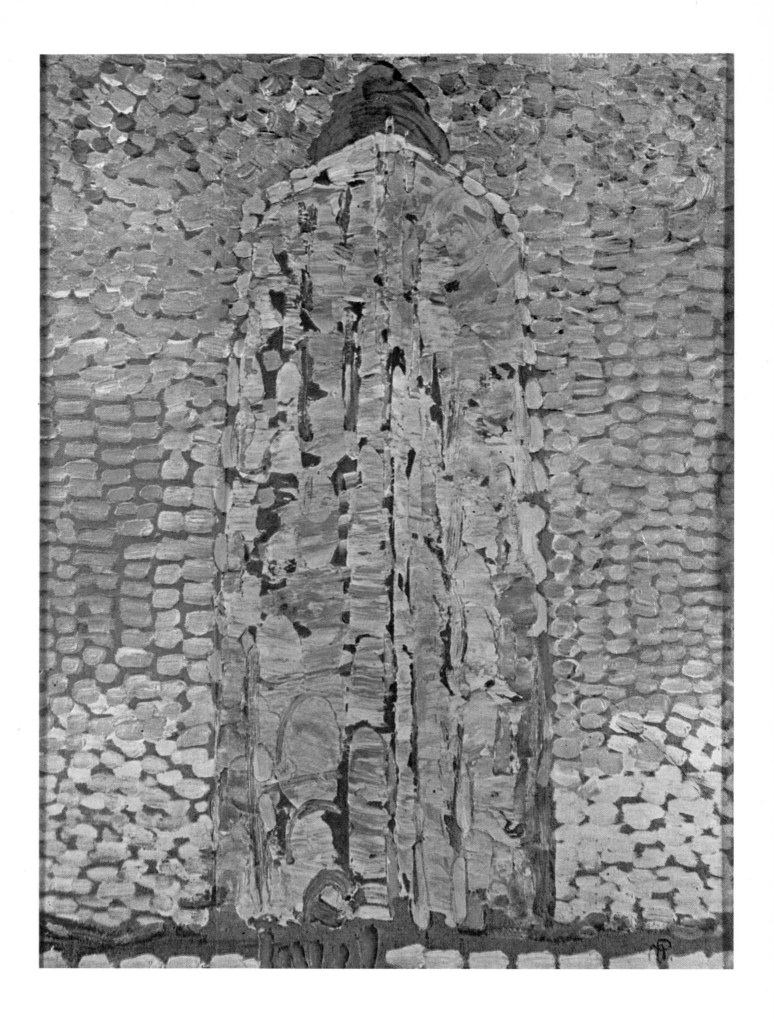

WASSILY KANDINSKY Composition
Water Colour Private Collection

PIET MONDRIAN Lighthouse, Westchapel
◁ Gouache Beyeler Gallery, Basle

OSKAR KOKOSCHKA   Reclining Woman   Pastel   Private Collection

EDVARD MUNCH Crouching Woman Water Colour Private Collection

MAURICE DE VLAMINCK   Landscape with River
Water Colour   Museum of Art, Basle

ANDRÉ DERAIN   Almanac (July) ▷
Sanguine   Private Collection

Ibels and Bottini bear sympathetic, sometimes bitter witness to a particularly problematic era while some others — and not only minor ones — have tried to serve an idea or a moral conception rather than a pure aesthetic.

The important function of these artists as illustrators rather than " pure " painters has naturally led them to adopt the methods with which this book is principally concerned. Humorous reviews accepted them simultaneously with the newcomers who were later to become famous for their skill in a less specialized and less emotional art. Many of them contributed to *L'Assiette au Beurre* (*The Buttered Plate*) among other, similar journals, as did many artists unknown at the time, including Jacques Villon and Juan Gris.

On the other hand the freedom towards which the impressionists and their immediate successors had pointed the way involved such enormous problems and such a vast scope that many artists plunged headlong into uncharted country. Seurat had tried to bring order into impressionism, and divisionism — his own invention — was adopted by an important group which included two outstanding water-colourists — Signac and Cross — and other skilled artists like Petit-Jean, Dubois-Pillet and above all Augrand and Maximilien Luce, who found this discipline an effective basis for their work.

Gauguin and Van Gogh, also born into impressionism, tried to go still further, and thinking they were prolonging this movement in fact started the process of its obsolescence, if not its actual destruction. Fauvism, with its strong, pure colours, grew from this desire for progress which was more easily expressed in terms of oil-painting. Many of the great artists who exemplify a trend inexpressible in terms of drawing and water-colour have in fact contributed vitally to the history of their development in this century from outside the movement itself, and even after it had lost its attractive, intriguing novelty.

Two names at once spring to mind — Matisse and Dufy — both mentioned earlier as particularly typical because they discovered formulas entirely suited to these techniques, and different from those they used in oil-painting. Matisse's drawings fall into two categories. He uses pencil for certain portraits and particularly for a series of voluptuous nudes, and indicates space by sculptured, varied shading of his surfaces. In his line-drawings he uses only the sweep of a stroke, without shadow or hatching, with an utter purity and great luminosity, and yet succeeds almost miraculously in creating the illusion of volume, space and texture. Matisse's drawings certainly belong among the greatest triumphs of modern art.

Raoul Dufy's drawings can also be divided into two groups: those which by simplicity of line, calm wisdom and deliberate frankness appeal to popular imagination and are easily made into wood-engravings, and those which by contrast are so nervously executed, so inventive and so full of lively detail that Dufy has conveyed in them impressions as fleeting as those created by the impressionists in painting — the movement of waves, the trembling of leaves, even a burst of light. Often the expert freshness of these drawings is perfected with touches of water-colour which blend so perfectly that it is hard to tell which process has priority. Apart from these drawings, his water-colours (in which the brush-work *is* the drawing) are exceptionally fresh, brilliant and light, in such perfect accord with his talents that one even won-

ANDRÉ DUNOYER DE SEGONZAC   Seated Woman
Pen and Ink   Museum of Modern Art, Paris

ders whether their colour harmonies, transparent textures and lightness of mood have
not deeply influenced Dufy's oil-painting.

Among the Fauves, Vlaminck's water-colours are worth mentioning, in particular those of his post-Fauvist period, when Cézanne's influence is most marked and
shows in washed landscapes where his fiery spirit and taste for texture find expression in strong blues and greens in sensuous contrast with the white of sky or snow.
Friesz also has a taste for strong, positive statements, whereas Laprade has produced
water-colours of a quiet lyricism, in gentle shades of grey, and drawings of a trem-
ulous femininity.

Throughout his life, Derain displayed the severity of his classical temperament, even when he was giving rein to his imagination and to the audacity inherent
in his haughty nature. Van Dongen belongs historically to Fauvism and deserves a
place of honour here for his brilliant, transparently luminous water-colours, which
burst with life and equally well belong to expressionism, because he in fact forms a
link between these two French and German trends.

The merits of water-colour and drawing compared with those of oil-painting
appear most strongly in the work of those artists whom one usually classifies as minor
masters, but whose gifts show to best advantage in this field, earning them a place in
the first rank for their assured inspiration, accurate observation and subtle sensitivity.
Painters such as Manguin, Valtat, Camoin, Jean Puy and Auguste Chabaud show
undisputed qualities in water-colour and drawing, in which they demonstrate a less
aggressive, modified form of Fauvism, no less rich, but in keeping with the times.
These artists establish clearly discernible links with the impressionist past. They all

CHARLES DESPIAU Seated Youth Sanguine Beaux-Arts Museum, Basle

FERDINAND HODLER Study for «Enttäuschten» Pencil, Indian Ink and Water Colour R. Bühler Coll., Winterthur

ANDRÉ MASSON   Grass and Flowers
Indian Ink   Louise Leiris Gallery, Paris

José Clemente Orozco   Study   Charcoal on Yellow Paper   Museum of Art, Philadelphia

Raoul Dufy

RAOUL DUFY Portrait of Jean Cocteau
Pastel H. Gaffié Collection, Beaulieu sur Mer

64

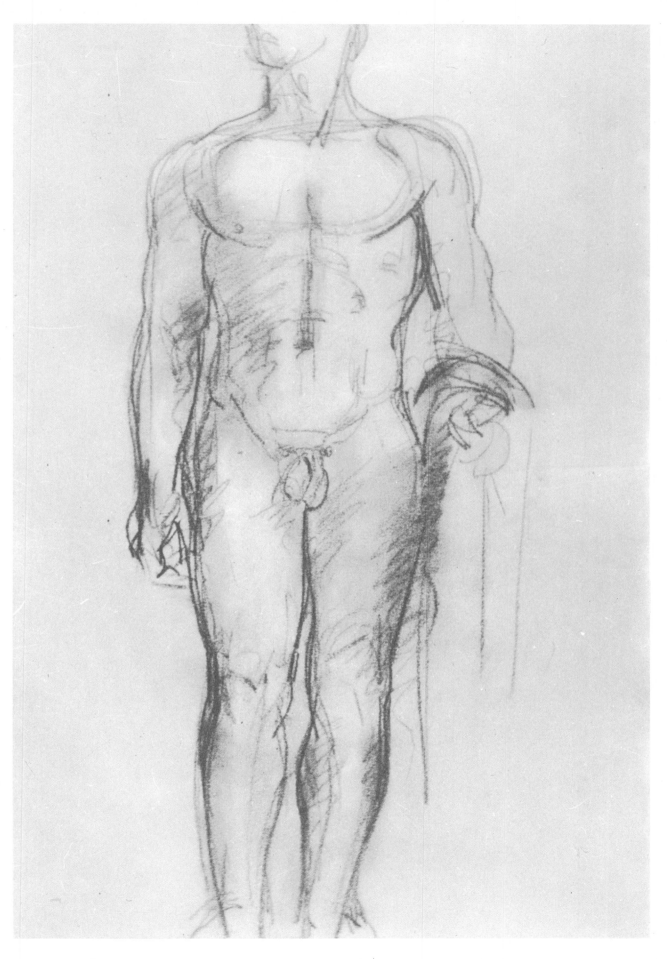

CHARLES DESPIAU Study for « Apollo » Sanguine Museum of Modern Art, Paris 65

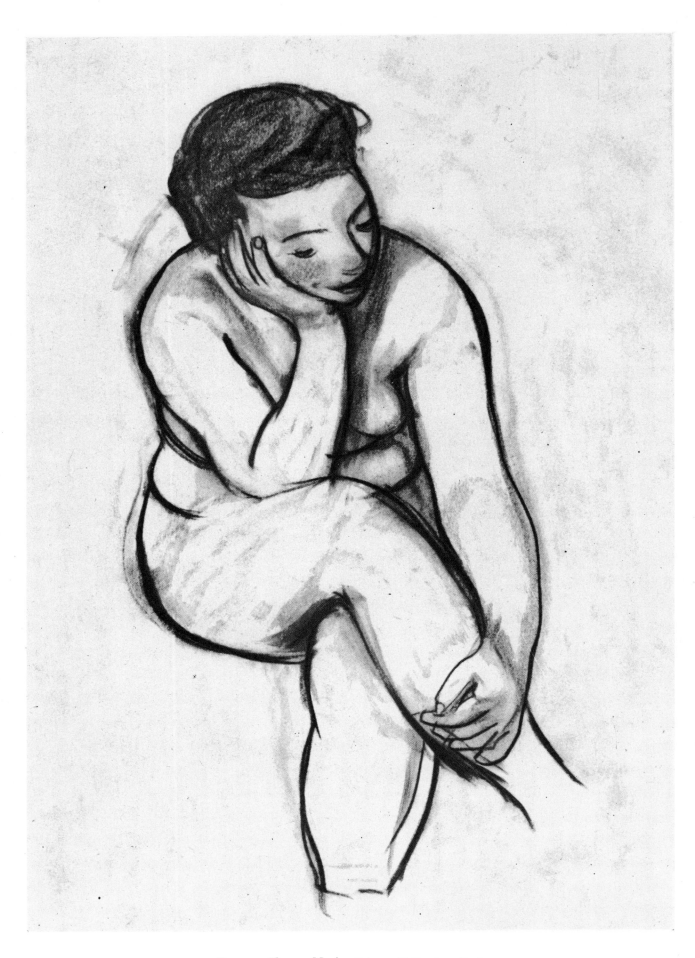

GEORGE KARS Nude Private Collection, Paris

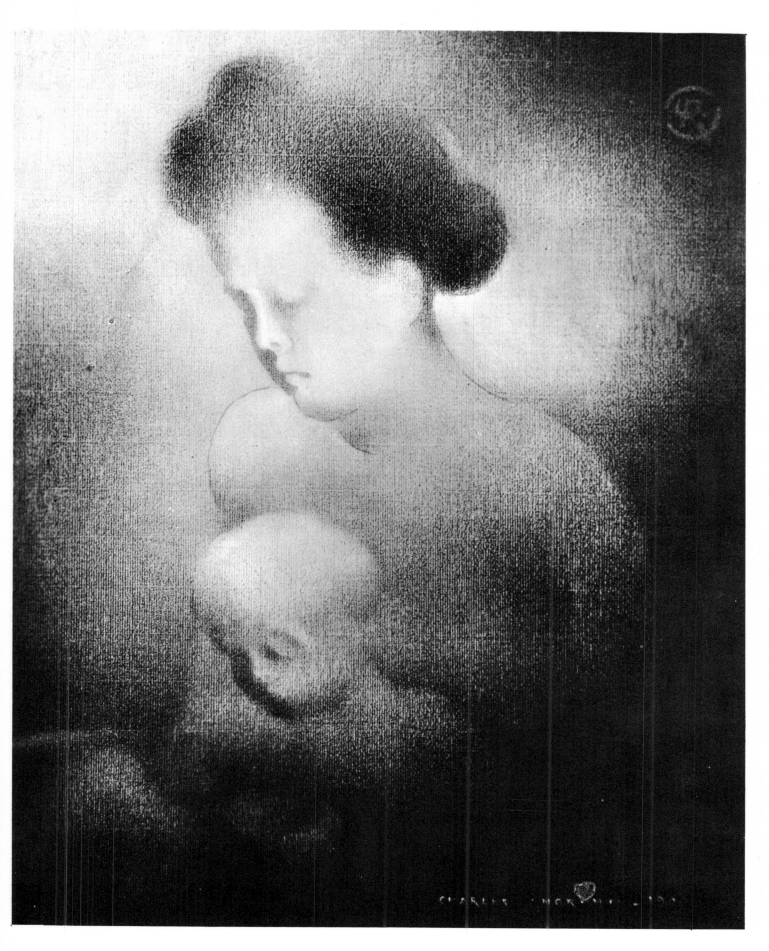

CHARLES ANGRAND   Maternity   Charcoal   Private Collection, Geneva

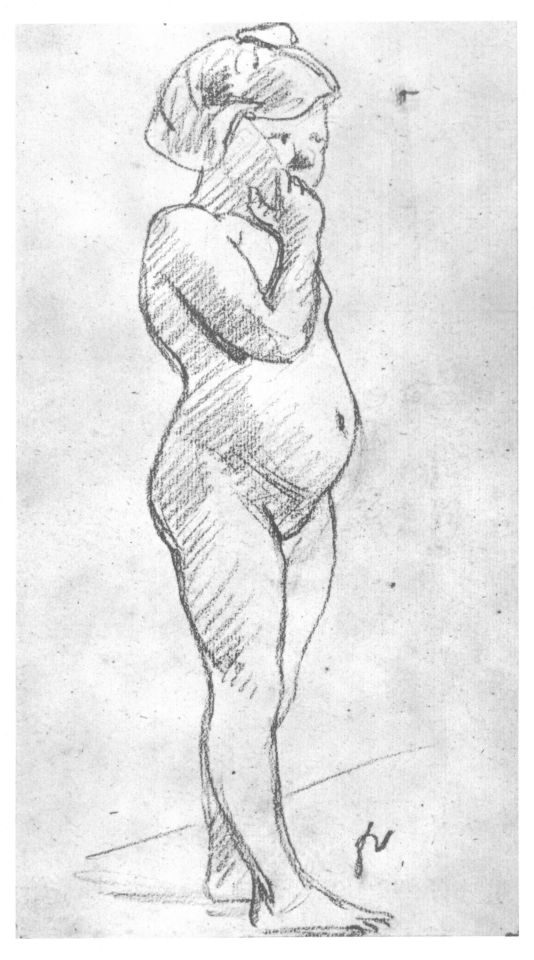

Félix Vallotton
Child Study
Sanguine
Richard Bühler
Collection, Winterthur

68

show a liking for feminine subjects, which they treat with great charm and an attractive sensuality, all, that is, except Chabaud, who exhibits an almost expressionistic violence in his work and on the whole prefers to paint his lovely, austere Provençal landscapes.

EXPRESSIONISM AND JEWISH PAINTING

In France the violent reaction against academic conventions which began around 1910 took the form of successive opposition movements which verged on the outrageous: first fauvism, and shortly after, cubism. Meanwhile similar trends were developing in other countries where, though not engulfed by the first lap of impressionism, artists also tended towards extravagances. In Germany artists of the Berlin group called " Die Brücke " (" The Bridge ") were as prominent as the fauves in subordinating form to colour, but they went further than the French in linking drawing with painting. The majority were very prolific in their work, not only in drawing but also in engraving, especially wood-engraving, where their love for stark contrast found expression in the harsh, exclusive use of black and white. Outstanding in this group were Kirchner, Nolde, Schmidt-Rottluff, Pechstein and Heckel. Several years later in Munich the artists Alexei von Jawlensky, Macke and Campendonck, calling their group " Der blaue Reiter " (" The Blue Rider "), were to emphasize this violence still more, particularly in their human figures, and to carry caricature to its limits in over-emphatic portrayal of emotion, while the Fauves and cubists only tried to express pictorial problems.

Ensor in Belgium and Munch who came from Scandinavia had already carried the function of the picture beyond mere landscape and still life and made it relate a comic or dramatic story. This tendency to add the pathos of an event to a painting as such was to find new impetus in the contemporary physical circumstances of the drama of war and the chaos which ensued throughout Europe both for the victors and the vanquished.

German expressionism is more than an aesthetic trend; it is a moral attitude, the consequence and mirror of the collapse of a society, its disciplines and its inhibitions. It marked this era so deeply that countless artists can be associated with it (apart from the members of the two groups already mentioned) and not from Germany alone, such as Beckmann or Otto Dix, but also from what is called " la peinture juive " (" Jewish painting "), a term which applies less to the temperament of a certain ethnic and religious group than to a trend almost exclusively confined to painters in Central Europe and Russia. This is in fact no racial phenomenon, but the melancholy eruption of human exasperation with former restraints, which when abruptly released was identified with the period of despair through which these artists had just passed. Soutine is the foremost and most powerful — but by no means the only — outstanding figure in this school. Later Kokoshka was also to attain a harsh dramatic grandeur in his analysis and caricature. In the realm of drawing alone, a special place must be assigned to Kubin's haunting fantasies of monstrous insects threatening mankind, and in drawing and water-colour to Schiele, who even in his gentler moods shows an astringent attitude to humanity.

Before the war in Germany there existed a group of original, acid caricaturists

JOHN SLOAN Model Asleep
Pencil Private Collection, New York

under the sobriquet " simplicissimus ", and after the war this trend was revived, in a form aggravated by circumstances. George Grosz, draughtsman rather than painter, was a pitiless, ferocious critic of contemporary absurdities and evils. His skilled, expressive draughtsmanship is sensitive, flexible and as candid as a bronze engraving. Several artists working in France showed similar, but less cruel tendencies, for instance Charles Laborde, whose powers of observation and graphic style were not without elegance, and above all Pascin, an astonishing artist, whose lines are like slender threads, exceptionally sensitive and expressive in the smallest details. Although these two artists were not French by origin, they in fact belong to the Paris school which began to attract a number of foreigners to Montparnasse. They gave a personal quality of vision to the post-war world, less despairing than that of the Germans, but no less disillusioned — a less sharp, less censorious vision, but yet one which embraced disturbing extremes. Another, contemporary example of this school of expressionism is Goerg, who was also a pitiless observer of a disintegrating

HENRI MATISSE Still Life
Pen and Ink Museum of Modern Art, Paris

HENRI MATISSE Odalisque
Pen and Ink   Museum of Modern Art, Paris

ANDRÉ DERAIN   Seated Nude ▷
Sanguine   Legacy Mrs. Meredith Hare, Museum of Modern Art, New York

73

MAURICE LOUTREUIL   The Guitarist
Charcoal   Museum of Modern Art, Paris

society with its exaggerated vices. Through his drawings Goerg became one of our best engravers, and one of the great modern illustrators, notably of Baudelaire's works.

In this same period Yves Alix belongs to the expressionist movement, but to him it was only a passing phase, as his feeling for balance drew him swiftly into a more disciplined art-form, not determined solely by its subject. The more spontaneous compositions of his later period should not be allowed to obliterate the memory of his earlier, incisive observation of humanity.

Perhaps Gromaire, generally considered the greatest, is in fact the only true

74

Félix Vallotton Clemenceau
Indian Ink Richard Bühler Collection, Winterthur

CARL BURCKHARDT Male Nude Study Sanguine Richard Bühler Collection, Winterthur

Franz Marc   Two Horses
Tempera   Rhode Island School of Design, Providence

EDVARD MUNCH   Standing Woman   Coloured Crayon   David Daniel Collection, New York

OTTO MUELLER Two Nudes under the Trees Water Colour and Crayon Kurt A. Körber Coll., Hamburg

AUGUST MACKE The Yellow Coat Water Colour State Museum, Ulm

French expressionist, because of his connections with Flemish expressionism which differs greatly from the German. But even Gromaire is in turn different from the Flemish. His distortions, or rather the spontaneous style he gives the people in his drawings, is not intended to exaggerate or heighten their moral character, but to mould them firmly into his general composition. In so doing, he comes nearer to the structural experiments of the cubists than the caricatures at which the expressionists aimed, yet he is not trying to dismember actual form like the cubists, but to give it positive strength through simplification. Among later artists, Armand Nakache revealed in his obsessive, exaggerated style his deep misgivings about the modern world.

It is usual to assert that French expressionism does not exist, and it is a fact that no group of French artists goes under that name. However there are many isolated examples, and if one considers them together one sees that they provide an outstanding and representative sample of this movement in France. One should include not only those already mentioned, but logically also Soutine and most of the Jewish artists of the school already referred to, such as Mané Katz, Kikoïne and Kremègne, who found in Paris a liberal focal point for assessing the past and for embarking on new ventures. As for Gen Paul, who belongs to no group, his wit and style as much as his subjects justify placing him in this context.

Above all Georges Rouault, one of the great masters of modern art, belongs here. By his style, his subject-matter, his wit and his passion he is an expressionist rather than a Fauve, as he is usually classified. His water-colours are certainly the most intense masterpieces and bring glory to modern art. The boldness of his technique and the grandeur of the emotions he portrays, whether in the faces of Christ, of clowns, of judges or of prostitutes, often remind one of Rembrandt and set Rouault apart as a genius. Here one should mention Bonhomme's water-colours, which are very similar to those of Rouault.

One great artist who belongs to French expressionism, Louise Hervieu, is largely forgotten to-day, but should be included here because she has almost wholly confined herself to black-and-white drawings. Her strange compositions — interiors cluttered with knick-knacks, hangings, flowers, feathers and nude women — which are as sumptuous and mysterious as romantic fantasies with deep shadows and gleaming reflections, set her apart from all " schools ". Charles Walch's drawings are spontaneously simple, tender yet rough, with clear colours, and his water-colours are in the popular vein of imagery. To a more recent generation belong painters like Clavé, whose water-colours are as dense as oil-paintings and whose figures are of towering stature.

In the paragraph on Gromaire, mention was made of Flemish expressionism, which in Belgium unconsciously acquired a slightly limited, peasant outlook, in contrast with German expressionism, which is healthy and robust both in its very positive style and in its colours. Permeke is the outstanding personality here, with his broad, strongly-built figures, and after him come Gustave de Smet and Edgar Tytgat, who emphasize the essentially popular character of this movement with a naïvety, which though artificial shows a certain freshness and skill. James Ensor is the grand old man of Belgian expressionism, but with a wholly different approach and style.

KARL SCHMIDT ROTTLUFF Head of a Girl Graphite Private Collection

82

ERNST LUDWIG KIRCHNER Two Couples Black Chalk and Pencil Staedel Art Institute, Frankfurt

84

FRANZ MARC   The Gazel
Water Colour and Gouache   Museum of Art, Rhode Island

ERNST BARLACH   Kneeling Woman
Black Chalk   Albertina, Vienna

LUDWIG KIRCHNER   Two Women on a Sofa
Water Colour   Dr. Max Ficher Collection, Stuttgart

86

EMIL NOLDE   Café (After Manet)
Wash and Indian Ink   Fogg Art Museum, Cambridge, Mass.

His contorted scenes of ghosts and masked figures heralded at the beginning of this century both the coming expressionism and the more remote surrealism.

In Brazil, some aspects of Portinari's strong personality link him with expressionism or cubism, and above all demonstrate the awakening of that country to the great problems of modern art, and its entry into the field with an artist of the first rank.

Finally Mexico, whére natural independence and revolutionary power are shown in works which can also be connected with expressionism and which in the space of half a century have given an exceptional character to its art. Three names typify this evolution of a powerful national movement — Diégo Rivéra, Siqueiros and Orozco. Around them artists and engravers have created a most individual black and white art-form. Younger than these artists, Ruffino Tamayo carries Mexican art beyond national limits, with oils and gouaches of a dramatic and poetic intensity which defies classification and can equally well be placed with expressionism, surrealism or abstract painting.

◁ ALEXEJ DE JAWLENSKY   Medusa
Gouache   Fine Arts Museum, Lyon

89

LOVIS CORINTH Self-Portrait
Black Chalk Fogg Art Museum, Cambridge, Mass.

EMIL NOLDE Couple Dancing Indian Ink Ada and Emil Nolde Foundation, Seebüll

First the impressionists, then the fauves and the expressionists, pursued an increasingly revolutionary course in the cause of liberating colour, broadening horizons and rejecting obsolete tradition. Once their aims had been achieved — by what seemed at the time drastic measures — this approach was bound to attract a reaction in favour of austerity, discipline, pictorial construction and a rediscovery of classical rules, but only while respecting the revolutionary spirit which had invaded artistic centres with increasing violence and romanticism in the first ten years of the century. Cubism, born in about 1907, was the direct product of this desire for severity, coupled with the urge to create a scandal in the name of a new artistic order. As it grew in opposition to fauvism (which stressed the dominance of colour) cubism placed its emphasis on construction, and therefore on draughtsmanship. In the period which ensued, Braque and Picasso created pictures in a very restricted colour-scale, almost monochrome, in order to stress the bones of their experiments. Drawing is so pre-eminent for the cubists that even later when they renounced this austerity they preserved precision of outline in their most colourful creations and somehow made their pictures look like coloured drawings.

Picasso's works, through all his varied periods, have great significance in this context. Drawing is so important to him that he has explored all its potentialities, either in creating minutely detailed portraits in the manner of Ingres, or indicating a complex composition with thread-like strokes, or playing with dots, lines, shading and blotches — a range he reinvented to discover how far he could go in exploiting the various resources of each chosen method.

Also in the works of Léger, though in quite a different way, draughtsmanship is in evidence in the thick outline around almost all his figures and objects, rather in the manner of the painters with whom he has been compared. Drawing is so important in the work of the cubists that they can all be cited as examples. Jacques Villon, though mostly concerned with making his colours glow and vibrate, can also be distinguished by his precise, yet never arid, draughtsmanship. Marcoussis has given us some outstanding plates and used his gifts equally in the field of engraving. Juan Gris shows a taste for linear work even in his oils. Albert Gleizes invented a style of composition which depends on the austerity of drawing. Férat's and Valmier's gouaches and water-colours depend less on texture than on draughtsmanship. André Lothe is more natural, more relaxed and more alive in his drawings and water-colours than in his oils. Marie Laurencin, who belongs to this movement more for emotional than aesthetic reasons, also accepts the primacy of design.

Once cubism had lost its first explosive impetus as an innovation, its adherents preserved their memory of its contribution to their work, that is, the refashioning of the world according to a complex geometry. Even among those who reverted to a more realistic style and sought a less arbitrary approach, one can still detect the trace of a certain simplification — a way of reducing volume to plane and of using colour in broad flat patches, which emerges particularly satisfactorily in gouaches. La Fresnaye creates most moving figures in this way and later on Hayden was also to find a simple, precise style for his lofty and generous landscapes, which however still vi-

LYONEL FEININGER   Aquaduct   Water Colour   Mrs. Lyonel Feininger Collection, New York City

PAUL KLEE   Landscape. The Past
Water Colour   Private Collection

RAOUL DUFY The Butterfly Ballet
Gouache Henri Gaffié Collection, Beaulieu s/Mer

MAURICE UTRILLO Montmartre: Le Passage Cottin
◁ Gouache Henri Gaffié Collection, Beaulieu s/Mer

97

SAYGY FIKRET, MOUALLA   The Musicians   Gouache   Modern Art Foundation, Geneva

ANDRÉ DERAIN   Carnaval People   Water Colour   Romanet Gallery, Paris

MOÏSE KISLING   Fishing Harbour   Water Colour   Private Collection

DUNOYER DE SEGONZAC   Still Life
Water Colour   Private Collection

THÉOPHILE STEINLEN The Happy Wanderer
Pastel Private Collection, Geneva

ANDRÉ PLANSON   Kitchen Interior   Water Colour   Museum of Modern Art, Paris   103

brate with light and convey the density of their spaces. Survage evolved a decorative formula and enlivened huge areas of solid colour with vivid, sweeping strokes.

Maria Blanchard and to a greater extent Metzinger were deeply influenced by the austerity of cubism, while Loutreuil and Favory gave more rein to their physical sensations.

Yet another field in which the cubists showed the importance they attached to drawing was their paper montage — a wholly cubist invention with which they succeeded in reconciling elements of disparate material appearance, and in which drawing is used as a linking agent.

Cubism marked the final break between photographic reproduction and painting, by asserting the artist's right to refashion the physical world, space and perspective according to his own private vision. It was an episode of destruction and reconstruction which affirmed and proved the necessity for a new approach, in which intelligence should govern sensuous perception. By its very existence it released all the movements which have subsequently challenged artistic ideas. The first example was to be found in Italy in 1911, started by artists attempting to portray or indicate the essential components of the new way of life. They called themselves futurists, thereby professing their intention of turning their backs on the past and blazing a path for the future. The new and especially modern elements of life which they portrayed were noise, light and above all movement in its ultimate form, that is, speed. Starting from the cubist assumption of the right to reconstruct forms, they then deviated to the extent of making their constructions dynamic, rather than static. They also considered draughtsmanship indissolubly bound to colour.

Seen from this point of view, futurism's aim, which was to animate a painted surface, found a parallel in France in the art of Robert Delaunay, who also started from very definite, precise forms, but through his use of contrast and colour harmony tended towards a vivid radiation of tone. Larionov and Goncharova followed a very similar course in their colour effulgence.

This emphasis on geometric forms to emphasize the structure and composition of a picture, which was vindicated by the cubists' success and which Amédée Ozenfant carried to the " purest " possible conclusion in absolute immobility, was taken up in other countries as a basis for systems much more rigid than those envisaged by its inaugurators. For example the Stijl movement in Holland and the Bauhaus in Germany were both derived from these principles and became the starting points for a movement which incorporated painters' ideas in a much more general aesthetic, embracing not only sculpture but the decorative arts and architecture, thereby placing on new foundations the problems of modern aesthetics in general and of the whole framework of life. When the German political regime violently attacked all aspects of modern art, the authors of this trend were forced into voluntary exile and most of them went to America, where they founded an ideology from which after several years there emerged abstract art, whether in Kandinsky's impulsive, half-defined shapes, or in Mondrian's and Malevitch's more definite structures.

PAUL KLEE   Rose-Coloured Form
◁ Pastel and Crayon   Private Collection

KAETHE KOLLWITZ Fettered Man Pen and Wash Erich Cohn Collection, New York

GIACOMO BALLA Moving Forms Pencil Private Collection

108

BÉLA CZÓBEL The Road Water Colour Private Collection

GEORGES ROUAULT   Girl in Blue   Water Colour   Romanet Gallery, Paris

Léon Bonhomme   Seated Woman with a Hat   Water Colour   Modern Art Foundation, Geneva

RAOUL DUFY The Reception Gouache Henri Gaffié Collection, Beaulieu s/Mer

UMBERTO BOCCIONI The Water Carriers

Pen and Ink Private Collection, Milan

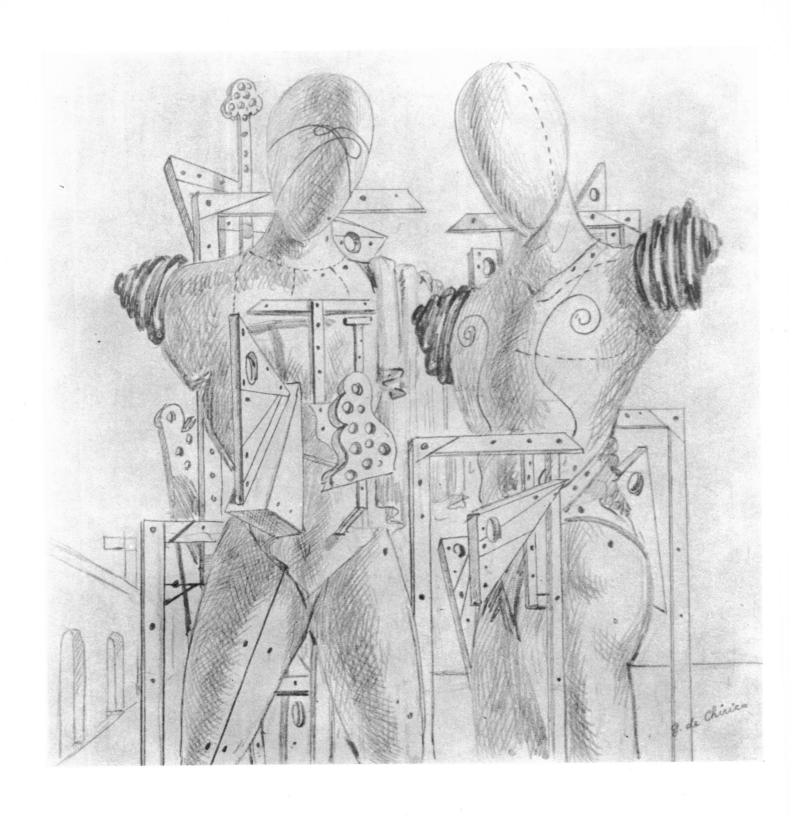

GIORGIO DE CHIRICO Metaphisical Design
Pencil Private Collection

114

ASPECTS OF REALISM

The powerful spread of cubism and subsequently of abstract art by no means suppressed the faithful disciples of realism, who were so numerous and obviously vigorous between the wars, though without any academic allegiance, that one might have thought they had won the fight and forced the aftermath of cubism into the background. They succeeded both in profiting from the lessons of the past and in avoiding mere imitation. Probably it was the consequences of the 1914 war which gave the then realism its very individual nature.

Even in the most dynamic moments of fauvism and cubism — that is, before 1914 and during the war — many artists succeeded in escaping the epidemic of new ideas and in standing aside from established schools of art, without falling into academic banality. Suzanne Valadon recalls Degas's classical figures in the strong lines of her characters and their precisely emphasized outlines. Modigliani invented for himself a style which owes little to the modern taste for distortion, except for a certain elongation of his figures and his female nudes, which may equally be an evocation of Florentine elegance of the Renaissance. Kisling also simplifies and purifies the contours of his women. Utrillo's predilection for squalid urban scenes revealed an intense poetry in despised landscapes. In fact between the wars this need for maintaining contact with reality, and especially with nature, spread in various ways while keeping pace with the current emotional climate.

Impressionism had become too remote and too placid for an era characterized by the recent drama of the 1914-18 war. Segonzac and his friend Luc-Albert Moreau could not forget the tragedies through which they had lived. The vehemence of fauvism seemed to some misplaced and futile after these actual events. Cubism was too systematized and too cerebral to satisfy those who needed a return to more familiar environs. Aside from some tentative sorties from the current trend which, as they had no lasting effect, may have been motivated by snobbery, most artists tried to realize a certain expansiveness in the calm serenity and sober joy of the new-found peace. The need for order called more for good taste than for bold adventure. To content oneself with everyday life and its peaceful harmonies it was necessary to draw a mental curtain before the recent upheaval while retaining a clear recollection of it in the depths of one's mind. The surrealists, the successors of cubism, were the only artists to pursue with unflinching relentlessness the search for an unrealistic art impelled by violent sensations. On the whole taste was tending towards a more undemanding and simply human satisfaction.

Segonzac and Luc-Albert Moreau were still closely bound to reality; not however for lack of other experiences, because some of Moreau's drawings, in particular, show definite cubist influence. Boussingault was friendly with them and certain very distinguished artists belonged to their group, such as Gernez, who showed as much independence and skill in his water-colours, gouaches and pastels as in his oils. Launois and Mainssieux, both outstanding water-colour painters, whose works are in the hands of private collectors, could be described as initiates.

Other artists in this group merit wider recognition, but their relative obscurity is due to their limited ambitions and the modesty of their works. Dufresne's paintings show vague traces of cubism, but are more especially characterized by the influence of exotic legend on his imagination. Vergé Sarrat, Ceria and countless other

MASSIMO CAMPIGLI Two Friends
Pen and Ink Private Collection

CARLO CARRA War on the Adriatic
◁ Pen and Ink Private Collection

118

MARIO SIRONI
Study of a Man Taming
a Rearing Horse
Pen and Ink
on Gray-Green Paper
Private Collection
New York
▷

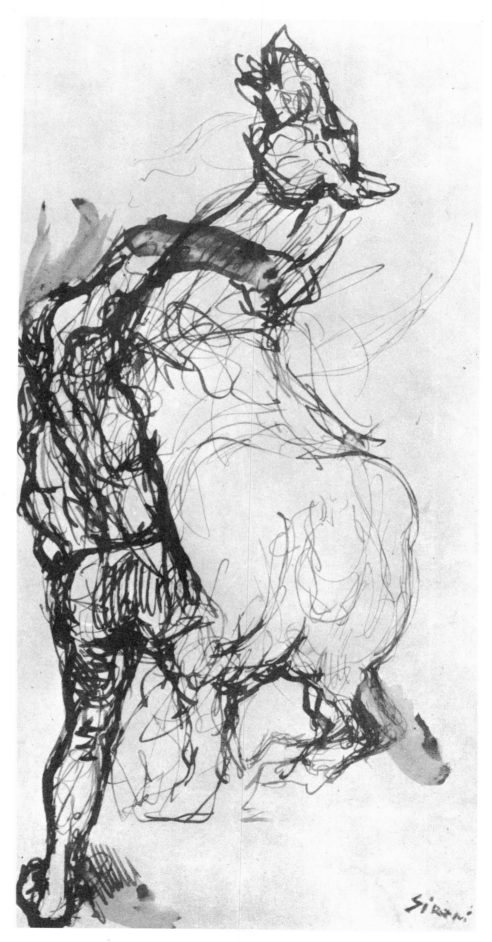

◁
LUIGI SPAZZAPAN
Horse
Indian Ink
B. Grossetti Collection
Milan

modest, sensitive painters, were in their time the stars of the Salon d'Automne and later of the Salon des Tuileries, and gave to these two exhibitions a vibrant, human atmosphere.

To these names can be added many others; Gromaire (who has already been mentioned); François Desnoyer, whose bold, vigorous and frank water-colours may have benefited from cubist or fauvist theories but only retain their intensity and none of their distortion; Pougny, who after subscribing to the beginnings of abstract art in Russia found a less stereotyped expressive mode in France and invented for his gouaches and his oils a technique of applying colours in small spots, which restored a vividness and intimacy reminiscent of Vuillard; La Patellière, who rediscovered a gravity and poetic dignity of a solid, rather rustic kind. As with Segonzac and most of the artists already mentioned, drawing is to him as much a serious task as painting; Kars's feeling for ample forms and solid draughtsmanship shows an affinity with Valadon's art.

This movement towards rediscovering nature became even more coherent in the following generation, and was adopted as a school of thought by many artists, though it did not immediately assume the character of a collective, organized movement, because it grew from mutual affinities, with no label and no manifesto. Only a few years ago was it named " Réalité Poétique ". The main nucleus at first consisted of a trio of friends, Oudot, Legueult and Brianchon, who were then joined by Yves Brayer, Cavaillès, Limouze, Terechkovitch, Caillard, Chapelain-Midy, Planson and Despierre. They painted a peaceful, smiling life remote from mundane considerations and nicely balanced between sensual pleasure and poetic intimacy. This balance seems more weighty in the works of Aujame, Rohner and Humblot.

After the 1939-45 war a new movement appeared, favouring a certain degree of realism — a movement more marked than the previous one by the feelings aroused by the war, and this time not reflecting a relaxed state of mind but one troubled to the point of being dubbed " misérabilisme " by its enemies. Drawing claimed an important place in this movement, of which Francis Gruber can be called a forerunner. Before the war he predicted man's anguish in an epoch of cruelty. His most expressive drawings show emaciated figures delineated in a few aggressive, harsh, candid strokes like scratches. The same troubled pity in a different style can be found in the works of Bernard Buffet, who swiftly attained widespread fame for his most spontaneous, assured style, which always stresses drawing as opposed to actual painting.

Minaux at first followed very much the same lines, but soon returned to a more relaxed, individual style, often in scenes of rustic inspiration. Jansem's mordant style depicts tortured lives and troubled and pathetic faces. Aïspiri often achieved most sumptuous effects in his water-colours. De Gallard portrayed the melancholy poetry of desolate slums. Commère, in spite of his sharp style of drawing and his broken lines, reveals a more relaxed attitude to nature, like Béllias who also loved to paint landscapes in which light threw planes of perspective into relief without contrasting them, and like Guiramond, Cathelin and Brasillier, who also subscribed to a generous, colourful mode of painting. Rebeyrolles started his career as a neo-realist

JEAN DUFY Still Life with Flowers and Glass
Watercolour Private Collection ▷

120

André Derain Festival
Water Colour Romanet Gallery, Paris

122

MARC CHAGALL   Nude   Pastel   Romanet Gallery, Paris

LOUIS VALTAT   The Tuileries
Water Colour   Romanet Gallery, Paris

TSUGOUHARU FOUJITA   Young Girl Seated ▷
Water Colour   Oscar Ghez Collection, Geneva

SAYGY FIKRET, MOUALLA   Animated Street
Gouache   Private Collection

GEN PAUL   14th of July
Gouache   Private Collection

126

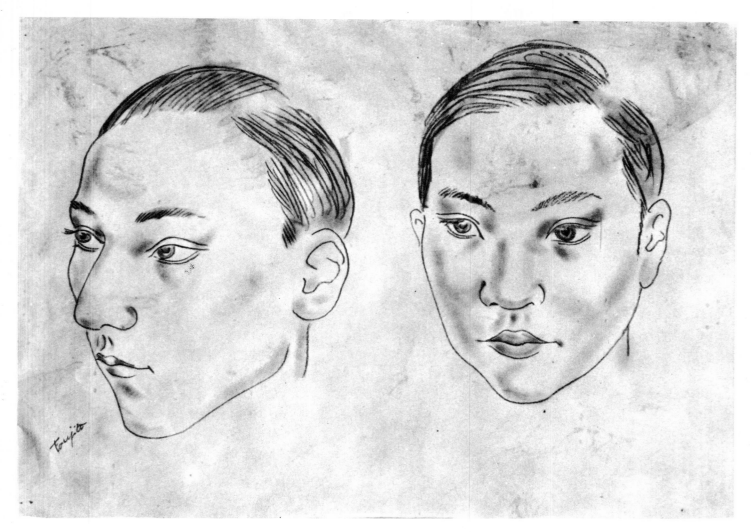

TSUGOUHARU FOUJITA   Two Asian Heads
Pen and Wash   Private Collection

and tried to carry his passion further. He was at first drawn to a personal form of expressionism which led him into an almost abstract idiom, where his violent temperament can be discerned, but not the sources of his inspiration.

Perhaps it is too arbitrary to mention Pignon here, for he in fact does not belong to any group and his forceful expansiveness and power of evocation are too individual to allow him to conform to the tenets of any " school ". He is always deeply impressed by the most basic aspects of life — the heat at harvest-time, the sensuality of a cock-fight, the ruggedness of tree-bark — and finds their plastic equivalent in countless water-colours executed on the spot, which he then transfers into oil-paintings. Jean-Jacques Morvau's work is in a similar vein, dominated by his almost obsessive preoccupation with sea and fire.

The Italians, hoping to create a strong national school in accordance with the

◁ MARIE LAURENCIN   Portrait of a Woman
Pastel   Museum of Modern Art, Paris

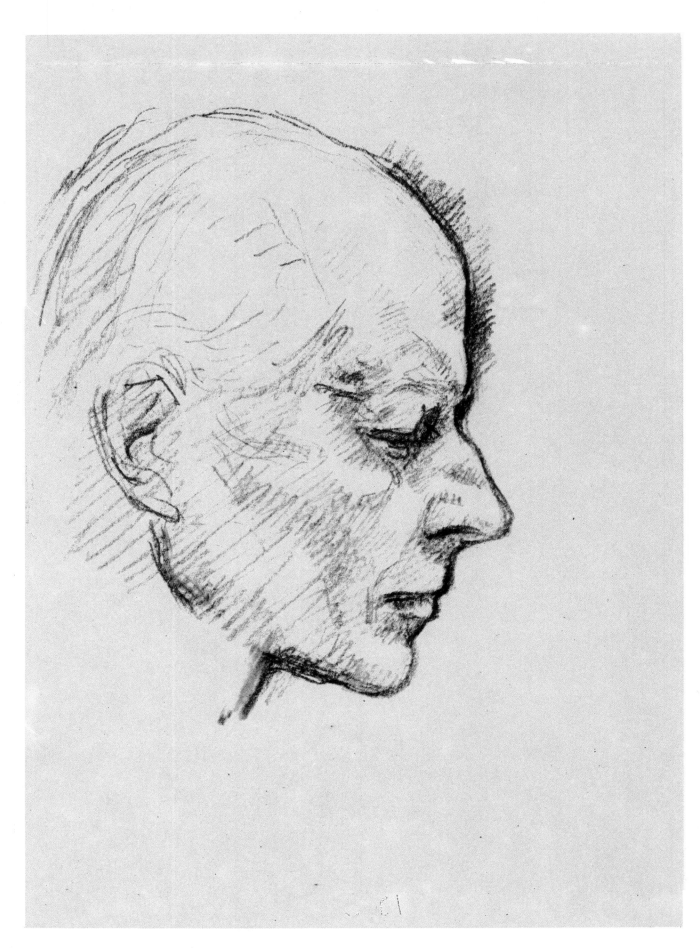

BENI FERENCZY   Portrait of Bela Bartók   Pencil   Private Collection

GIACOMO MANZÙ Head of a Young Woman Brown Chalk Arrigo Lampugnani Collection, Milan

ideals of its political regime, held aloof from the great international trends, but several artists escaped from these limitations. Morandi, for instance, with the amazing harmony of order and poetry in his quiet still lifes; De Pisis, with his landscapes and still lifes brilliantly and nimbly executed with a few acutely sensitive strokes in a style for which water-colours and gouaches are the ideal media, and Campigli, whose delicate, refined paintings evoke the exquisite materials and tones of old frescoes. In the post-war period there has also been a movement of popular realism, notably in the works of Guttuso.

The defence of realism took on most varied, not unpoetic forms in the U.S.A., ranging from Hopper's static density to Ben Shahn's contorted characters with their disturbing gestures, and including Marin's spacious and lively simplicity, which is sometimes classed among abstract art.

In Switzerland exact drawing, for instance Hans Enri's sketches, was of a traditional nature, rightly avoided the academic label and showed a leaning towards surrealism. Auberjonois was a tranquil, sensitive painter. He drew austerely and betrayed both memories of cubism and a certain naïve severity like the Flemish expressionists. Adrien Holy had lived for some time in France on intimate terms with " the poetic realists " and Cuno Amiet, after a brief involvement with the German avant-garde movement, settled into a moderate, calm style, in which he could still exploit the effects of light and shade.

POETRY AND INTELLIGENCE: SURREALISM AND ABSTRACT ART

By continually striving to avoid imitating reality and to stress the spiritual significance of the universe, modern art has been inexorably drawn to invade the domain of poetry and has willingly followed a parallel course of development, because both written and verbal poetry at that time sought to avoid too much precision. In two of its aspects modern art is closely linked to poetic expression: firstly in its surrealism, secondly in its abstractions. These two forms of expression, even if apparently connected or even overlapping, are in fact very different in their aims and often also in their achievements.

One must primarily remember that chronologically surrealism's fame and public following preceded that of abstract art, the latter having attained its greatest development after the second world war, while the former was launched and reached its peak a few years after the 1914-18 war. The poetic aims of surrealism are so obvious that it never formed an aesthetic school but a stream of thought, and its most outstanding exponents have all devised or adapted different and even opposed aesthetics. It is enough to mention the names of the most famous surrealists such as Dali, Max Ernst, Tanguy, Miro, Masson, Brauner, Picabia, Valentine Hugo and Léonor Fini to understand that their affinity depends on a particular manner of observing the communication between the outer and inner world, while each painter interprets his own perception in different ways.

Surrealism is no specially topical phenomenon, isolated and cut off from the past. On the contrary, not only is it possible to find parallels in earlier centuries, but even to-day it existed before André Breton had postulated its theories and organized its development. Artists like Chagall, de Chirico and the exponents of Italian

metaphysical painting around 1915, let alone Picasso, were obviously its precursors, because some of their works represented an invasion of the realm of the poetic, the wondrous and the logically inexplicable.

The surrealist painters explored this vein with imaginations fertile in finding new images rather than new media of expression, because in most cases they adopted familiar techniques but demanded of them startling effects. They even brought skill in materials to the point of touching on an academic didacticism. This was especially true of Dali, Tanguy and the French cubists, or of Delvaux and Magritte in Belgium. Others, particularly Max Ernst and Schwitters, have experimented with new processes and explored the unexpected in every direction. Their collages, *frattages* and engravings show their continual concern not to confine themselves to traditional formulas. All this passes the bounds of oil-painting and touches on either drawing or the assemblage of different materials, the effects of which the cubists had already tried to exploit some years earlier, though for plastic rather than poetic purposes.

GIORGIO MORANDI   Still Life with Glasses and Pitcher
Indian Ink   M. Del Corno Collection, Milan

The springs of surrealism were not exhausted by its inaugurators, for younger disciples appeared to prolong the movement, such as Matta, Vilfredo Lam and several others who created a hypnotically forceful universe, like that of the Englishman Graham Sutherland.   In the final event the greatest contribution to the expansion of surrealism by the use in gouache or water-colour of its techniques for transfiguring reality were made by the less involved surrealist painters such as Lucien Coutaud and even Carzou, who was in part realistic illustrator and in part a purveyor of legend.

Inasmuch as they care to vitalize a stylized reality, some surrealists are of course the heralds of abstract art.   Others who have maintained their independence (and many of whom had already been noticed for some years for their figurative art) belong to the no-man's-land which goes unacknowledged by either figurative or abstract painters and yet is open to various innovations, although these artists do not

HENRI LAURENS Nude Pencil Private Collection, Paris

easily compromise. Painters like Bissière, Tal Coat, Manessier, Singier, Zao Wou Ki,
Vieira da Silva, André Marchand, Lapicque and Borès, let alone Dubuffet, grew in
this atmosphere and poetic realm, where the plastic resources not only express physical sensation in terms of space, form or colour, but also a spiritual atmosphere, which
by referring back to reality remains more accessible to the public imagination than
wholly abstract art. These artists move gradually away from cubism, fauvism or

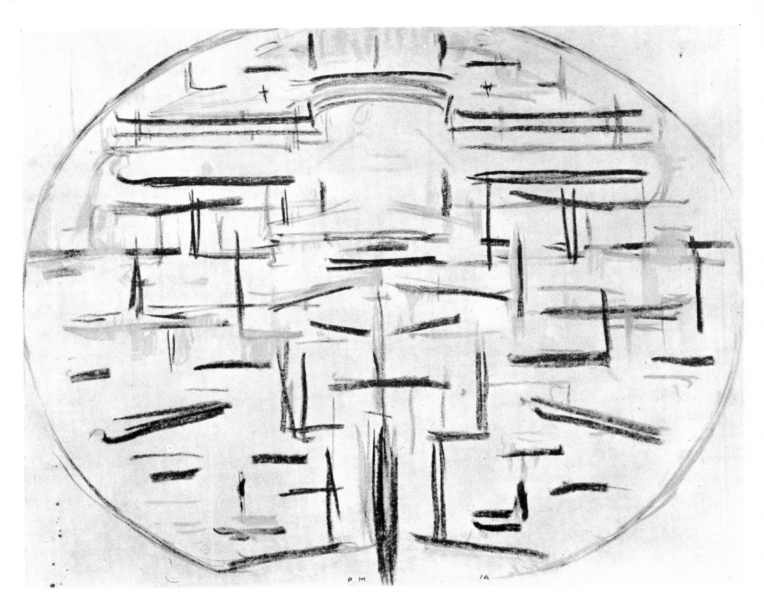

PIET MONDRIAN Pier and Ocean
Charcoal Beyeler Gallery, Basle

impressionism, while conceding membership of those movements, and preserving the effects of that first influence which had so deeply permeated their personalities, whether cubism, as in the case of Roger Chastel and Geer van Velde, or impressionism as in the case of Garbell, Cottavoz and Bolin.

Abstract art was able to achieve its liberty openly, thanks to cubism's rejection of photographic reality. Its uncompromising desire for purity gave its materials and graphic style a sure validity. Dubuffet's art resembles graffiti, but significant graffiti, such as caricatures of personalities. Wols's art is in a similar vein but in a wholly emancipated idiom, abandoned to the dangers of improvization. Graffiti (instinctive

FERNAND LÉGER Composition
Water Colour Romanet Gallery, Paris ▷

136

AUGUSTE HERBIN Arabesque
Water Colour   Mr. and Mrs. Isadore Levin Collection, Palm Beach, Florida

ANDRÉ LHOTE Still Life Water Colour Museum of Art, Basle

GEORGES VALMIER   Still Life with Fish
Gouache   Modern Art Foundation, Geneva

140

MARCEL GROMAIRE Nude
Pen and Ink Mr. and Mrs. Isadore Levin Collection, Palm Beach, Florida

JACQUES VILLON   The Three Magi
Pen and Ink   Museum of Modern Art, Paris

drawings) have of course the richest potential range of expression because, whether consciously or not and without subscribing to any rule, they portray inner movement all the more clearly for striving to reflect a sensitive external perception. Graffiti reached their highest level of sophistication in the work of Paul Klee, where it is hard to distinguish between consciousness and intuition, science and instinct. Klee's work has an infinite capacity for growth and novelty, because he finds in drawing, often with the finishing touch of water-colour, an endless variety of ways to escape

JACQUES VILLON   Corneille
Pen and Ink   Louis Carré Gallery, Paris

from existing aesthetic systems and pursue the continuously shifting changes of dream images. His work is poised at the furthest limits between figurative art and abstract art.

Beyond the work of Klee, one finds oneself in a wholly imaginary world, whether because the artists have mastered and can therefore communicate their impulses, as in Wols and Bryen's blotchy style, Fautrier's subtle evocations, Hartung's and Soulages's strongly instinctive slashing technique, Reichel's dreams, Nicolas de Stael's rough assertions, Lanskoy's sonorous brilliance or in many of Kandinsky's works, or because, on the contrary, the artist has followed reason and theory towards a much more positively constructed art, like that of Mondrian, Malevitch, Kupka, Herbin and Vasarely, or Piaubert's more flexible version, quite apart from Robert Delaunay and Sonia Delaunay who, however impulsive in their glowing play of colours, are ultimately governed by the geometric discipline of their rhythms.

In fact the duality in the Delaunays' art is fairly characteristic of the position of French artists, who occasionally adopt arbitrary solutions like Mondrian. In maintaining this balance, their art is no hesitation, but contains a deep wish to preserve the human element in the physical world. Even Mathieu, whose work seems wholly detached from physical significance, betrays by his subject-matter his concern with the portrayal of his own era in all its varied physical, spiritual and even metaphysical aspects. Poliakoff has no such problems, and his gouaches show an intense refinement of contrasting colour vibrations through the animation of great flat areas of solid colour.

The Americans are much more systematic in approach, though Tobey's gouaches and oils are far from improvized and his treatment of his surfaces is in effect an experiment in sophisticated innovation. Pollock himself succeeded in expressing the most complex emotions by empirical means. Most other Americans have for some years been only lightly touched by European influence. They have either turned in reaction to inspiration from the Far East, or confined themselves to original improvization, justified by the more or less exclusive use of abstract art. Examples of this are Rothko, Gottlieb, Kline, de Kooning and Sam Francis. Thereafter the Americans moved on to Pop Art — a violent example of the return to realism, which has attained great popularity among European artists.

Since the war Italy has become another stronghold of abstract art, but with more varied and delicate subtlety. The Italian rejection of influence is similar to that of the Americans, but could not entirely exclude the formers' exceptional heritage of erudite and skilled tradition. The Italian painters, however tempted to excessive licence after the restrictions of Fascism, could never revert to the somewhat impoverished simplifications of the Americans. Their sophistication led them rather into virtuosity and superficial effects. Magnelli is one of the best who was not led astray by such virtuosity. He succeeded in retaining the restraint of reason and the will to compose and arrange his forms while most of his colleagues in attempting lyricism often achieved only pyrotechnics.

In Holland colour experiments surpassed in violence those of other countries, as in the work of Appel, and extended expressionism into abstract art, with the Cobra movement and Jorn.

At any rate, by virtue of its emancipation of instinct, abstract art was the style nearest to poetry and made it possible for even those without any training in tech-

ALBERT GLEIZES Crucifixion ▷
Water Colour   Museum of Modern Art, Paris

Henri Matisse 2/42

146

JEAN METZINGER Two Heads
Gouache Oscar Ghez Collection, Geneva

HENRI MATISSE Young Girl at the Window, White Dress with Black Belt
Gouache Private Collection

Serge Férat
...an with Guitar
Gouache
...and Mrs. Isadore
Levin Collection
Palm Beach
Florida
▷

◁
Frank
Kupka
Composition
Gouache
Karl Flinker
Gallery, Paris

MAURICE DE VLAMINCK Landscape
Water Colour Private Collection

JOHN MARIN   Circus Elephants
Gouache and Water Colour   Alfred Stieglitz Collection, The Art Institute of Chicago

151

MARC CHAGALL   Sketch for « The Fire Bird »   Water Colour   Private Collection

nique to express their feelings in plastic form. Certainly before drawing became respectable poets had already found in it a way of portraying what they could not say, a way of indicating feelings which words would crystallize into too precise a definition. Max Jacob's drawings and gouaches are especially significant in this context and have a sharpness which is wholly in contrast with his poetic vision and even becomes aggressiveness, clearly discernible beneath his ironic prose style. Cocteau's drawings are equally visibly tormented and often more direct than his writing. One can even say that no poet of this period, from Paul Valéry and the Comtesse de Nouailles to Henri Michaux, did not attempt to convey their thoughts in drawing or water-colour as well.

SPECIAL TRENDS

THE PLEASANT LIFE
WOMEN, FASHIONS, THEATRE, INTERIOR DESIGN

We have still to mention those painters and works which do not belong among the main currents already discussed and yet contributed vitally to artistic life on the fringe of history. These are the painters who illustrate every-day life, reflect fashions and sometimes even create them. Their repute, however momentary, contributes to the history of taste, but art historians dedicated to defining and explaining major trends rather than to considering familiar details of a less essential nature generally ignore them.

In fact for more than a century artistic evolution as we study and teach it has depended originally on names and works at least with little connection and little success with the general artistic public, which therefore has not given them any great support. The major creations of modern art are all provocative gestures which at first aroused more hostility than praise. Appreciation started with a small group of intellectuals and connoisseurs whose mental endowments, assurance, and social prestige, together with the force with which they defended and broadcast their opinions, both compelled acceptance of their choices and gave their opponents a feeling of inferiority. Most of the general public has tended to follow the opinions of this élite minority, even when instinctively hostile to innovation, and thus artists whose works are readily and spontaneously accepted by the majority and hold the public's attention with ease, are often viewed with unfavourable prejudice by the experts. As a result, well-known painters of world-famous pictures are frequently deprecated or ignored by art-historians, which has caused the wide divergence between public and informed opinion — a divergence which since the middle of this century has become increasingly marked and unbridgeable.

Perhaps in explaining this divergence of opinion one should take into account the fashion for ideas, intellectual constructions and aesthetic formulas which so markedly characterizes the various stages in modern art and brings into the foreground those artists who willingly follow such trends, while those whose inspiration lies in simple every-day life in its pleasanter aspects cannot satisfy the current demands.

GIACOMO MANZÙ Seated Woman Study Sanguine Arrigo Lampugnani Collection, Milan

PABLO PICASSO   The Painter and His Model
Indian Ink   Private Collection

It does seem exaggerated, however, to ignore or exclude the latter, who do in fact most vividly evoke their period.   Gabriel de Saint-Aubin's drawings in the eighteenth century and those of Constantin Guys in the nineteenth are also a part of their

155

156

EMILE ANTOINE
BOURDELLE
Dancing Girl
Pen and Ink
Basle Art Museum
▷

◁
JULIO GONZALES
Maternity
Pen and Wash
Museum of Modern Art
Paris

time and are obviously not without charm and significance in recording customs and costumes. The painters of female elegance in our century are no more trivial, and their works can be referred to usefully and agreeably when studying contemporary life and taste, rather in the manner of book or magazine illustrations or even caricatures, though being specialized and detailed they are more reliable mirrors of their times.

One of the most remarkable groups of artists of this type is that which assembled shortly after the 1914-18 war around the *Gazette du Bon Ton* (*Gazette of Good Taste*), at a moment of extreme sophistication when the eccentricities of modern art started to have a snob appeal. The arrival of the Ballet Russes, the birth of cubism and the innovations of the couturier Paul Poiret contributed to a novel conception of feminine elegance. Pierre Brissand, Bernard Boutet de Monvel, Georges Lepapa, Marty, Martin and Brunelleschi stripped the aggressiveness from modern art and decked it in a new charm. They were all accomplished water-colour artists, some of them distinguished by a preciousness reminiscent of oriental miniaturists, while others revived the style of eighteenth century fashion plates and adapted it to modern taste.

After the war those artists attracted to feminine subjects were neither so stereotyped nor so superficial. Their humour and their delicacy were both more direct and more sentimental, and no longer dedicated to portraying fashion. The names of Pascin, Kisling and Charles Laborde arose in the chapter on expressionism because of the sharp, even cruel element in their imaginations, but they could equally well be included here, since this sharpness contains a considerable element of affection and even tenderness towards women. Dignimont's attitude is simpler, resembling the witty, amoral, but direct and open libertinism of the eighteenth century. His drawings touch delicately on eroticism, always in tender, non-violent tints. Touchagues uses similar subjects but seems rougher and nearer to popular painting. Foujita contributed an original note to the Ecole de Paris with his skilful, lightly shaded drawings whose elegance betrays their Japanese origins. By virtue of their chosen subjects as well as of their techniques, all these artists are infinitely more at home in water-colour than in oil, because oils make their idealized view of life too hard and material.

Among painters of women is one, Christian Bérard, who occupied a special place in modern art, eluded all classification and subscribed to no theories, in spite of his many friendships and considerable success among the élite. His supporters are also those who materially assured the spread of surrealism and helped first cubism then abstract art towards world fame. Bérard belonged to none of these groups, mingled with no major stream and never aspired to lead any school. His type of art is the least likely to interest contemporary critics, whether or not favourably inclined. He owes his success to his stage designs, magazine sketches and models for the great fashion-houses, though several beautiful portraits bear witness to his talents as a great painter, which he voluntarily sacrificed to these very ephemeral creations. His contribution to modern fashion trends is distinguished by lovely abundant drapery, cascading folds and elegant natural curves, when the tendency was all towards func-

JACQUES LIPCHITZ Figure 53
Water Colour Varenne Gallery, Paris ▷

RAOUL DUFY   Circus Horses
Water Colour   Henri Gaffié Collection, Beaulieu s/Mer

BEN SHAHN   The Dancers
Pen and Ink   Mrs. Lee Bunce Collection, Hartford, Conn.

MOÏSE KISLING   Rue de la Gaieté, Paris
Water Colour   Oscar Ghez Collection, Geneva

HENRI LEBASQUE Woman with Red Umbrella
Water Colour Private Collection

163

MARC CHAGALL   Flowers and Fruit
Water Colour   Mrs. Albert D. Lasker Collection, New York City

MAURICE BRIANCHON   At the Theatre
◁ Lithographic Inks   Private Collection

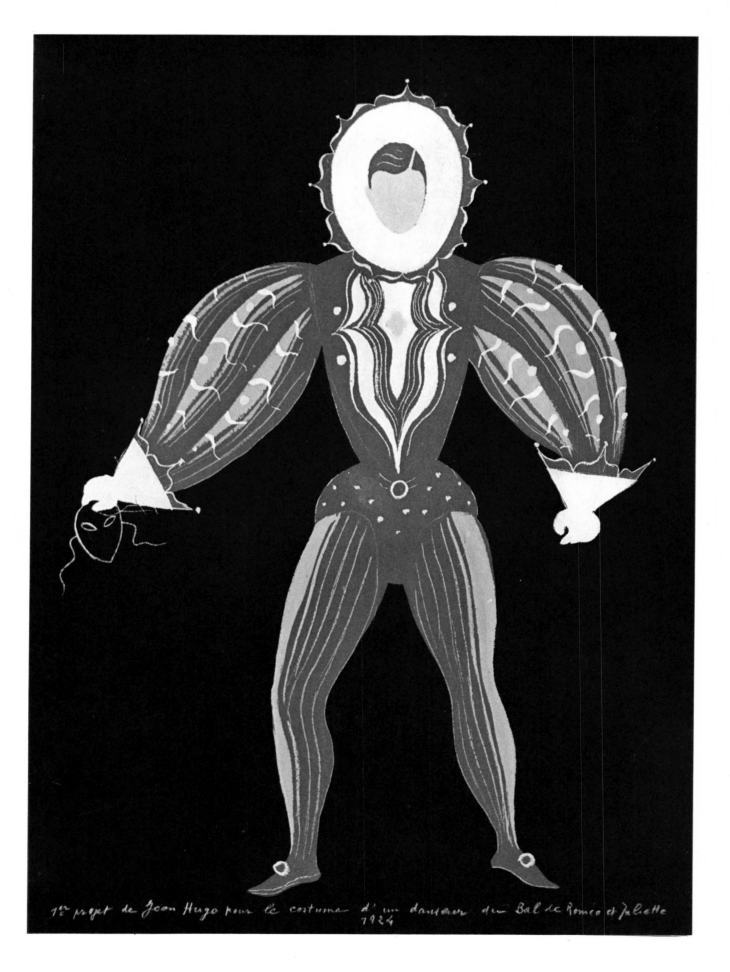

1ᵉʳ projet de Jean Hugo pour le costume d'un danseur du Bal de Roméo et Juliette
1924

JEAN LURÇAT Sun-Rise
Water Colour Museum of Modern Art, Paris

◁ JEAN HUGO Costume for " Romeo and Juliet "
Gouache Private Collection, Paris

DIEGO RIVERA   Mexican Girl   Gouache   Private Collection

JACOB EPSTEIN   Reclining Nude
Water Colour   Private Collection

169

ERNST WILHELM NAY   Composition in Yellow and Red   Water Colour   Private Collection

ERNST WILHELM NAY Composition Water Colour Private Collection

Béla Czóbel   Portrait of Mrs. Ferenczy
Pastel   Private Collection

WALDO PEIRCE   Nude Bathing   Water Colour   Private Collection

RENATO GUTTUSO   Sketch for the " Crucifixion "
Water Colour   Mario De Ponte Collection, Milan

MARIO CARLETTI   Pure Love ▷
Water Colour   Collection of the Artist

HENRY MOORE   Reclining Figure (Study for Sculpture II)   Water Colour   H. Pickering Collection, London

tional forms in costumes and furnishings, and the discovery of poetry and beauty in pure geometry. Fashion and the theatre gave him continuous scope for his ideas, and water-colour and gouache allowed him to improvize skilfully with supple brush-strokes which just touch the paper, leaving the hint of a curve and a suggestion of movement.

The special style of costume and stage design sketches is dictated by the need for exact models which the builders, painters and costume-makers could follow; hence precise drawings, flat expanses of colour and the almost exclusive use of gouache and water-colour, which obviate the temptation to create an effect of texture as one can in oil-painting.

The considerable success of the Ballets Russes in Paris in 1908 and the succeeding years was largely due to Serge Diaghilev's insistence on using original painters, and not specialist craftsmen, for his décor. The work of several great Russian artists was displayed in the first few seasons. Répine, Golovine, Korovine, Bilibine and above all Alexander Benois, later joined by Goncharova and Larionov, all demonstrated their own personal vision of oriental imagery. Greatest of all was Léon Bakst, whose sumptuous creations looked like illuminations. In the years that followed, the use of modern art for the stage was developed to include the most advanced artists. Picasso's and Derain's gouaches and Braque's water-colours for the modern theatre can count among those artists' most brilliant works in a realm and style very different from those of their pictures. Mention should be made here of the very important contribution made by Jacques Rouché, who as director first of the Théâtre des Arts, then of the Opéra, discovered several outstanding artists, notably Dresa with his rather precious eighteenth century elegance and Maxime Detomas, a lovely and powerful designer.

The theatrical revival after the 1914-18 war benefited from this trend, and many young artists took a special interest in theatrical design. Two theatre directors, Charles Dullin and Louis Jouvet, were conspicuous in their efforts to discover new talent (the latter in particular employed Bérard) and contributed largely to establishing this new style, which lay between imaginative painting and fashion-plate, while serving also as a record of their time. Artists such as Barsacq, Jean Hugo, Vakalo and Georges Wakhevitch have displayed most sophisticated originality and preserved a truly sensitive method of expression. Many of to-day's works in this style can be valued both for their decorative merits and as original gouaches or water-colours.

Beside the contributions in this field of the most famous names, such as Chagall, Dufy, Léger, Chirico and Dali, other painters have brought their gifts to the theatre, among them Brianchon, for Jean-Louis Barrault; Pignon, and especially Gischia, for Vilar; Chapelain-Midy and Yves Brayer. There are also a number of specialists in this genre, such as François Ganneau, Lila de Nobili, Bonnat, Suzanne Lalique and Suzanne Reymond — numerous enough to ensure a great variety of work — who have continued to enrich this important aspect of modern art without allowing it to deteriorate into mere craftsmanship, as it had at the end of the nineteenth century.

In the same innovatory spirit which led modern art to explore all related forms and gave new lustre to some less distinguished ones, was the discovery of tapestry, which demanded the exclusive use of gouache in a special style for executing the models. Jean Lurçat is the undisputed master and author of this reviving movement, but many other artists took part, from Jean Picart Le Doux to Prassinos and Adam.

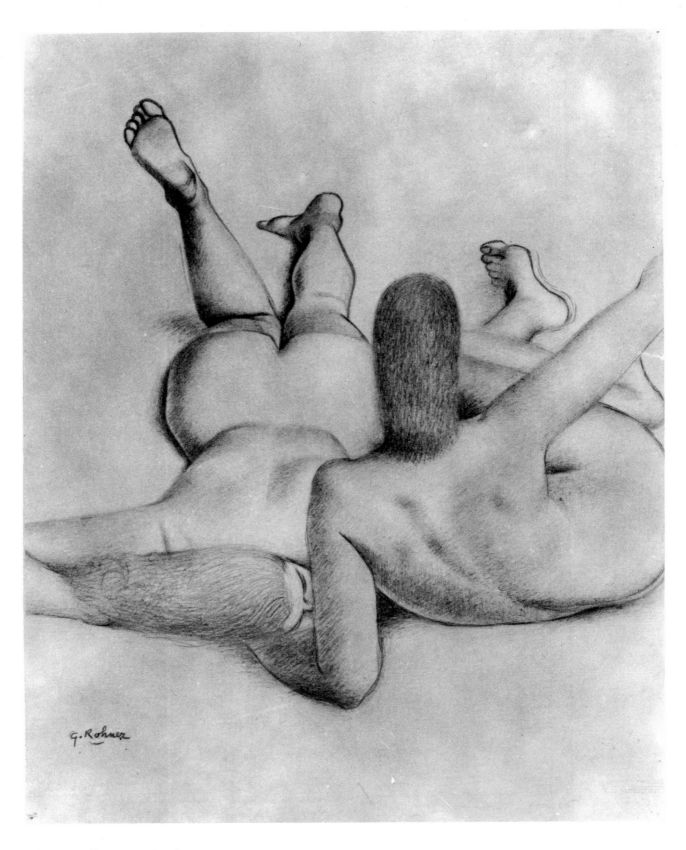

GEORGES ROHNER   Study
Pencil   Private Collection

FRANCIS GRUBER   Nude ▷
Water Colour   Private Collection

MARCEL GIMOND Head of a Woman Charcoal Private Collection, Paris

OSKAR KOKOSCHKA   Bouquet of Flowers   Water Colour   Private Collection

RAYMOND LEGUEULT   Interior
Water Colour   Private Collection

182

C. Terechkovitch   Young Girls on the Beach
Water Colour   Private Collection

This is a most cursory sketch of the field of theatre design, and has only dealt with France; the equally rich and widespread activity which has taken place in many other countries would need a fuller study. The idea here is only to link these activities with gouache and water-colour, to which these artists have contributed in considerable quantity and at a high level of quality and originality.

TECHNICAL USES: ADVERTISING, POSTERS

Drawing, water-colour and gouache have assumed such a wide independence and have so extended their field of activity that some realms now belong to them exclusively, as shown in the last chapter. As a result, the teaching of the graphic arts has become a very specialized and important branch of the artistic complex.

The illustration of books, reviews and journals exacts an intensive production of drawings and has helped in developing the caricature; to this must finally be added commercial art in all its forms, but particularly in advertising — one of the strangest and most singular of modern inventions. As the purpose of this book is to cover the drawings of painters and sculptors, this new subject will only be touched on in passing insofar as it is related to the work of painters, though it has an aesthetic of its own.

Commercial painting is in fact an offshoot of drawing, water-colour, gouache and even fresco, but not of oil-painting, which is usually thought of primarily under the term " art ". This is one of the first and main reasons for the independence of commercial art. Because of the wide public towards which it is directed, advertising is one of the most obvious forms of popular art, which had apparently vanished from modern life, and has now reappeared in unexpected ways. Like popular art, besides, advertising has coined its own, simplified language, both subtle and basic, using clear delineation, bright colours and easy symbols. It has even succeeded in creating personalities who have become famous or even legendary, such as Michelin's Bibendum for automobile tyres or Johnnie Walker for whiskey. This new mythology has become an integral part of our epoque and is as representative of it, or even more so, than its loftier masterpieces which are known and appreciated by an infinitely smaller public.

The most successful and talented commercial artists are rarely also known for their serious painting, yet their considerable skill cannot be denied. In the last years of the nineteenth century and the first years of the twentieth advertising was first launched and first attracted strong personalities, and from then on good painters devoted themselves to this work, and in general did not occupy themselves with the revolution in pictorial art. Among these publicity artists, some are however equally famous as " pure " painters, for example Toulouse-Lautrec (but the Lautrec of lithography, i.e. of drawing, and not the Lautrec of the oil-paintings), Bonnard almost by chance and equally as a lithographer, Vallotton to a certain extent, Maurice Denis

JEAN DUBUFFET
Portrait of Limbour
Charcoal
Mr. and Mrs. Isadore
Levin Collection
Palm Beach
Florida
◁

▷
FRANÇOIS DESNOYE
Dressin
Pencil and Was
Museum of Modern Art
Pari

ROBERT HUMBLOT   Seated Nude
Water Colour   Private Collection

BERNARD BUFFET   Head
Red and Black Chalk   Private Collection Geneva

Lajos Szentiványi Cannes
Gouache Private Collection

190

192

MAURICE BRIANCHON   Woman with Mirror
Pastel   Private Collection

UMBERTO LILLONI   Luna Hotel, Venice
Water Colour   G. Parozzi Collection, Milan

193

ANDRÉ DIGNIMONT Portrait of a Young Woman
Water Colour and Pencil Private Collection

C. Terechkovitch   Young Woman   Water Colour   Private Collection

196   RENATO GUTTUSO Head of a Woman Water Colour Bolchini Collection, Milan

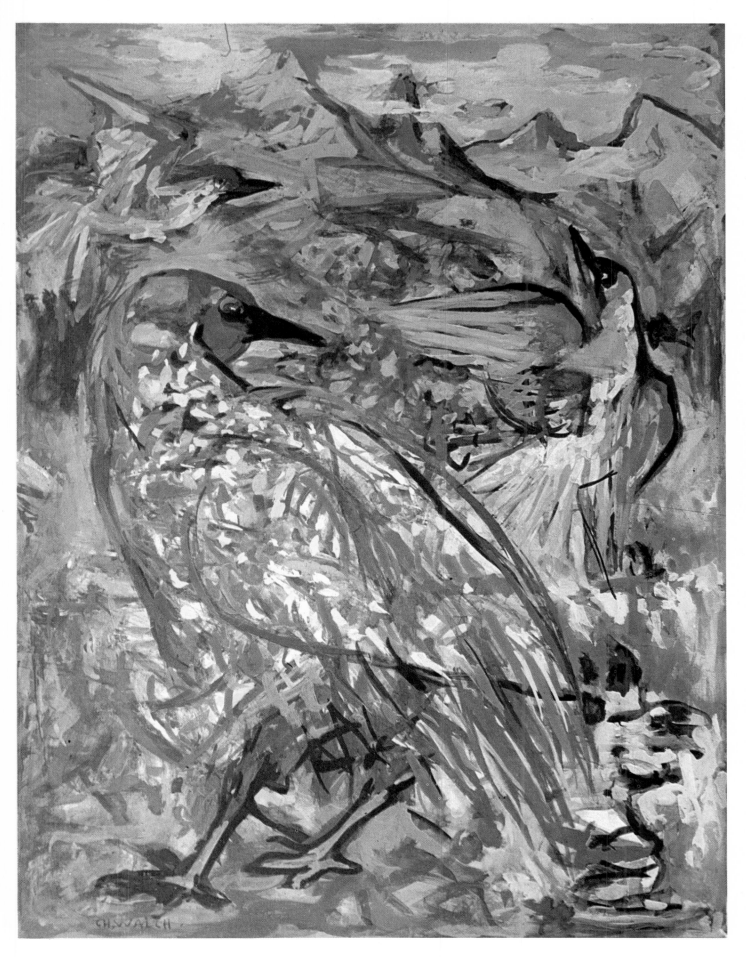

CHARLES WALCH Alpine Climber Water Colour Museum of Modern Art, Paris 197

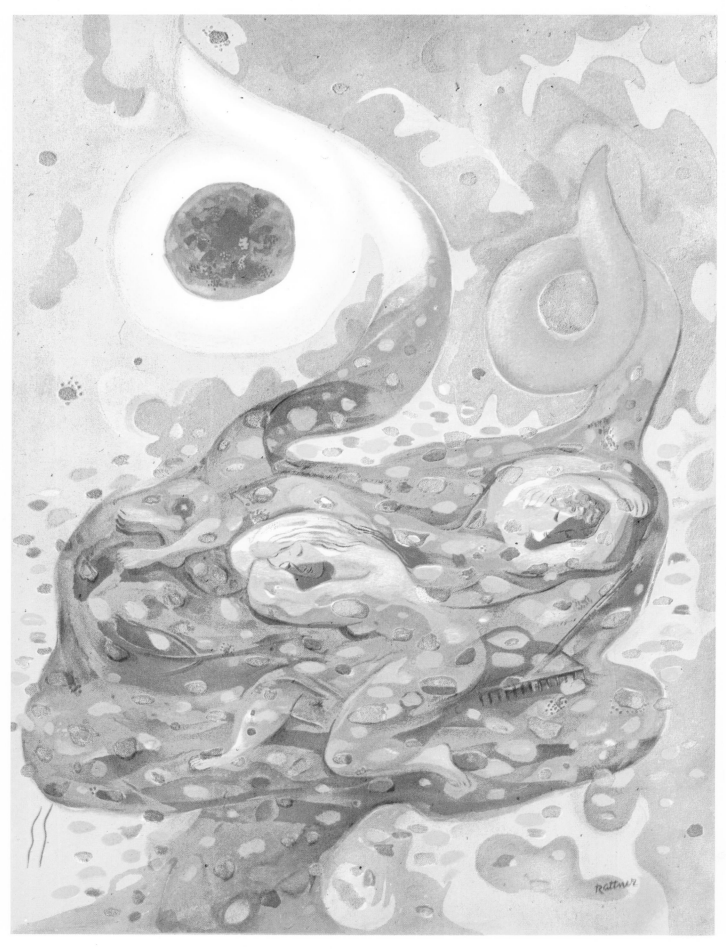

198   ABRAHAM RATTNER   Composition   Water Colour   Private Collection

JOAN MIRO   Composition   Gouache   Private-Collection   199

Serge Férat   The Circus Clowns
Water Colour   Museum of Modern Art, Paris

200

LUCIEN COUTAUD The Prodigal Son
Water Colour Museum of Modern Art, Paris

PABLO PICASSO   The Artist and His Model
Gouache   Private Collection

GEORGES BRAQUE   Still Life
Gouache   Private Collection

203

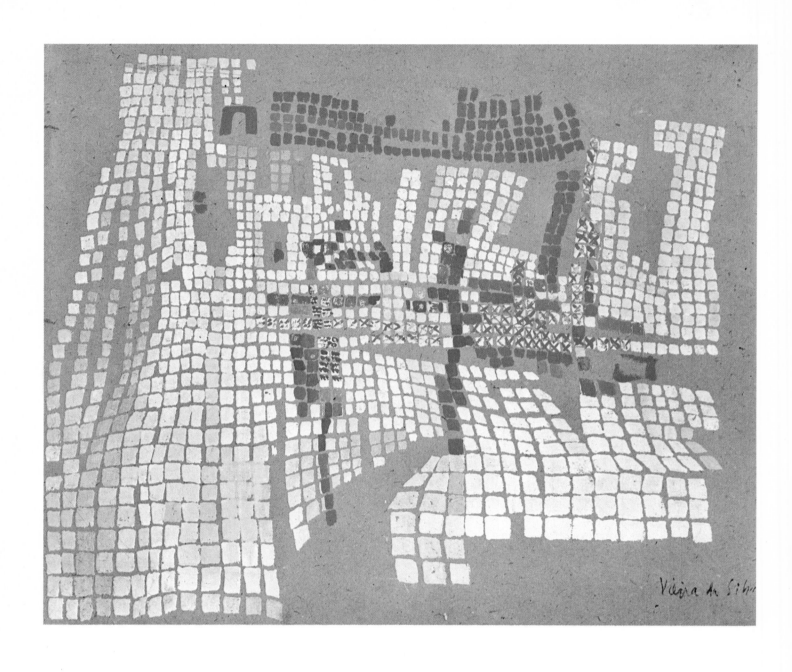

MARIA HELENA VIEIRA DA SILVA   Abstract Mosaic
Gouache   Museum of Art, Basle

204

Louis Touchagues
Portrait of Leslie
Caron Practicing
(15 years old)
Pencil
Museum of Modern Art
Paris

205

less so, and lastly Jacques Villon, but in a style very different from that which earned him his fame.

It would be inaccurate to deduce from this that the needs of advertising preclude the collaboration of great artists. Mucha, Grasset, Forain and Steinlein should not be underestimated. Each proved his originality by creating a personal style to suit the subject in hand, and each invented his own imagery and language as new as and often more skilled than most of those used by easel painters. All of them are principally designers, however, whether in sinuous curves like Mucha's, Grasset's and Feure's " modern style ", or in caricatures like those of Sem, Barrère, Josset, de Losques, Carlègle, Roubille or Veber, or in Forain's, Ibel's and Steinlein's mordant observation of mankind. Seuls, Chéret, Cappiello and Jules Grün use the technique of painters and adapt it successfully to the printing methods used in advertising.

These masters of the poster do not stand apart from other movements in the realms of painting, but often form a link between them with the necessary modific-

ANDRÉ MARCHAND   Study of the Sea
Indian Ink   Artist's Collection

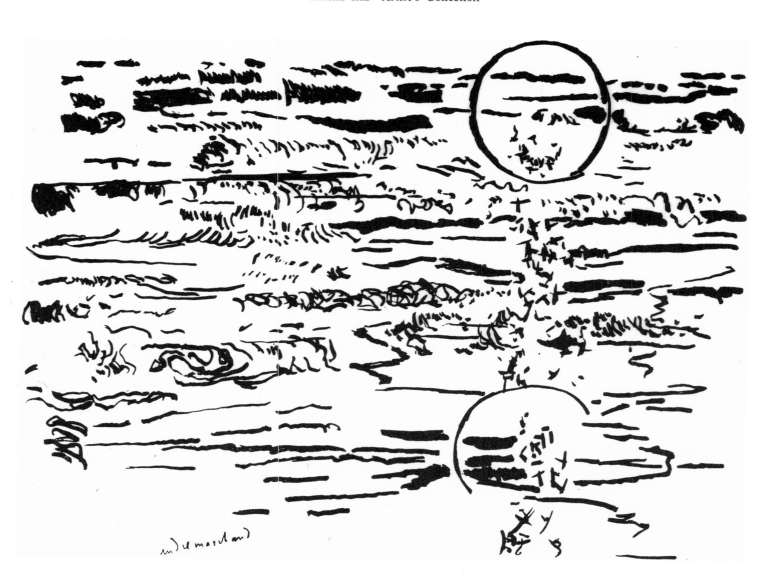

PIERRE TAL COAT   Large Drawing
Indian Ink   Museum of Modern Art, Paris

ations to different techniques. Steinlein's, Ibel's and Forain's sharpness of line and their resigned or blasé characters who reflect pity or repugnance, are in the Lautrec tradition. Chéret, Grün and Cappiello resemble the impressionists and their brilliant touch and glittering sweep of movement marks an extension of that trend. Josset, Roubille, Carlègle and de Losques are not simply caricaturists: their manner of outlining forms with a strong supple line and of using colour in large planes with a crude candour, would be nothing without the daring of the Fauves, whose pure, contrasting colours were bursting out on their canvases at the same moment. Mucha, Grasset and de Feure are a little affected and precious in a similar vein to that of the English and German movements, and Maurice Denis also uses certain harmonies which are supported by the *Revue Blanche* in its defence of Vuillard, Bonnard and Vallotton.

The great commercial artists join the great painters in the same type of endeavour when they undertake book illustrations, but not one of them is content with his rôle as illustrator alone, and their posters are not enlarged vignettes, but real compositions with all the mural qualities needed for these purposes.

Specialization is becoming so much more exclusive and despotic that commercial art is attracting and holding some great artists, the majority of whom are authentically painters. After the First World War a youthful team consisting of Carlu, Cassandre, Colin and Loupot started a real mural plastic art, in harmony with the new trends in painting. The following generation, including Villemot, Savignac and Roger Wild, tended towards a type of candid irony.

Advertising is thus developing parallel to and sometimes even apparently in opposition to what one calls " great art ", whether established or revolutionary, and is unconsciously defending more or less deliberately abandoned positions.

In a period when frescoes and murals are largely disregarded and development is almost exclusively confined to easel painting, advertising has by reason of its function, size, method of treatment and way of creating an appropriate scale, been the instinctive reaction — animating a surface without destroying its unity. In a period when subject-matter has been most eliminated in favour of pure art, advertising has on the contrary accepted its essential subordination to its subject, and proved that such subordination by no means excludes expression and the development of personality, nor a restrained boldness in research and invention. In a period when the artist has been shouting his independence at the top of his voice, advertising has demonstrated the creative potential of a type of craftsmanship, and of the possible, even necessary collaboration between client and painter, businessman and creative artist. In a period when other developing artistic expressions are content with, and even seeking, a limited public, preferring the reasoned appreciation of initiates, advertising has on the contrary set out to capture the largest possible public immediately, without demanding of it the least intellectual effort.

So by reason of its rôle in commercial art — for an advertising sketch is almost invariably a drawing or a gouache — an art-form previously regarded as secondary has acquired a prominent position in portraying every-day life.

SCULPTORS' DRAWINGS

In any history of drawing sculptors' sketches deserve a separate chapter, because their relationship with and contrast to the finished work are more definite than in the case of a painter. Above all the sculptor views his draft and uses its ideas in a wholly different way, whether it is executed in water-colour or monochrome, because even the application of colour usually differs from that of the painter, on account of its ultimate purpose. For the painter in oils, drawing and water-colour sketches are the first attempts to fashion disparate elements into some kind of order and to arrange on his given surface contrasting values which must be balanced if the surface is to have any unity or the spatial rhythms any cohesion. The sculptor, on the contrary, is working towards a concentration and portrayal of a mass, in which

MAURICE ESTÈVE   Composition 258
Indian Ink and Wash   Museum of Modern Art, Paris

each element, however lively and dynamic, must integrate with the mass and contribute to its overall character.

Even in the most radiant sculptures, like Carpeaux's " La Danse ", every part is integrally bound to the fundamental volume. Even in the most intense painting, as for instance Leonardo's " Mona Lisa ", or his " Virgin with Saint Anne ", the various elements diffuse themselves over the whole canvas.

A sculptor's drawings are of necessity bound to this basic, essential premise, without which sculpture cannot exist, and as a result drawing is as indispensable to a sculptor as to a painter, inasmuch as the latter can also take his first notes and make preparatory drafts and trial compositions, before attacking his definitive material.

Various factors determine the type of drawing or water-colour used by a sculptor. Point-drawing on the filiform principle as used by Rodin is more a suggestion of movement and spatial dynamics, which must then be translated into volumes to maintain its buoyancy. This is a hasty sketch, inspired and spontaneous, or a reflection of the artist's imagination. Secondly there is precision drawing, itself often

ANTONIO MUSIC   Composition
Charcoal   Gallery de France Collection, Paris

quite emphatic, which is a draft of the contours and limits of form and volume, as used by Gimond with strong intense outlines, or by Couturier and Volti with more flexible curves than Gimond and less movement than Rodin, without a finished elegance but as a precise indication of form. Laurens refines his lines with the utmost severity and plastic expression, and so creates a wholly definitive form. Adam's drawings look more like those of an engraver than a sculptor. Jean Arp's drawings are clear and simple like a diagram of a human body, and Pevsner's, though similar, are more complex, resembling living geometry.

Finally there is the moulded drawing, with shade and perspective, usually in monochrome and often in sepia. This is a precise draft of volume, in which the sculpture itself is already implicit, observed in its formal, progressive evolution. Maillol's sketches portray the tranquil voluptuousness of his nudes and Carton's show the lissom grace of his. Despiau's drawings betray the trembling sensuousness with which he invests his apparently simple subject, and Belmondo's betray a classicism free from banality. This cameo-style drawing is favoured by the majority of sculptors, no doubt because it approaches more nearly and can evoke the potential-

GUSTAVE SINGIER   Composition   Indian Ink   Gallery de France Collection, Paris

ities of the finished work, almost with the effects of a bas-relief. Gimond has said that a sculpture should be studied from every side and that each should lead one to assume the existence of something behind it. A bas-relief should show the nature of the finished work. Drawings like those discussed above are the nearest to bas-relief and offer an exact illustration of Gimond's definition.

It only remains to speak of the more complex compositions in water-colour; more complex, because the use of colour introduces a new dimension apart from that of actual space which is properly that of the sculptor. Colour however comprises also the play of light on planes, and its function of stressing them or leaving them unstressed. This accounts for the sculptor's involvement with colour, and one appreciates it vividly in Rodin's astonishing water-colours, which are not the work of a painter, but of an artist who felt the density of volume or movement and could express it in terms of colour. This ability is one of the rare revelations of true virtuosity in the realm of art, and shows that Rodin cannot be too narrowly classified.

Another example of the use of colour in a sculptor's sketches is afforded by Bourdelle. The drawings, but particularly the water-colours, which he executed for the Théâtre des Champs-Elysées are typical of his manner and demonstrate his wish to harmonize with the architecture and to fit his sculptures to its form and space. There is a monumental feeling in the smallest of Bourdelle's sketches. The colour itself is dull, like cement, recalling the frescoes in the foyer of the theatre. It strongly delineates large planes and plots movements, and its wealth lies in the restrained, concentrated force revealed in the limited palette, which never attempts effects of violently contrasted tones. This is all the more significant when one thinks that Bourdelle is a contemporary of the spread of fauvism and expressionism, and that with the exception of some of the cubists all artistic movements followed Cézanne in the same exaltation of colour. Bourdelle's water-colours are almost like cameos, and one feels that for him the essence lies in the suggestion of volume and the interplay of planes. This austerity in colour is not a constriction, but a good discipline. It prevents Bourdelle from falling into the expansive lyricism which one senses beneath this self-imposed severity. One is constantly aware of his enthusiasm about to burst through the barriers of reason and engulf the figures he portrays. His heroes are usually the gods of antiquity and myth, with symbolic significance.

The legend is more familiar in the case of Henry Moore, for his gods have resigned their thrones to human beings and topicality has succeeded symbolism. Nevertheless his works exude grandeur and tragedy. Moore was deeply moved by the intense tragedy of every-day events in England at a moment when banality had grown beyond the confines of a legend. For instance, in the bombing of London during the last war, he interpreted people sheltering in the dark passages of the Underground Railway as a human return to the chrysalis and a transformation into ghosts. One does not think of aesthetic problems or of the links between sculptor and draughtsman when considering these water-colours. Pathos, though never declamatory, dominates them all, but must be ignored if one is to see how Moore has used his visions of man reduced to anonymity in his search for plastic expression. Perhaps these uncertainly defined visions have not been without influence on his art. Here we face an exact example of a historical fact transfigured by emotion and by the professional insight of a sculptor, who reduces the individual to a symbol. Gon-

HANS HARTUNG   Composition
Pastel   Museum of Modern Art, Paris

213

GIUSEPPE
CAPOGROSSI
Composition
Gouache
Cavallino Gallery
Venice
◁

JEAN RENÉ BAZAINE   Composition
Water Colour   Private Collection

ALFRED MANESSIER   N. 9 in the Prairie
Water Colour   Museum of Art, Basle

CHARLES LAPICQUE Figure Indian Ink Villand and Galanis Gallery, Paris

OSSIP ZADKINE Head of a Man
Indian Ink Museum of Modern Art, Paris

◁ ALBERTO GIACOMETTI Figure
Water Colour Private Collection

zalès draws with a violent, realistic acerbity and maintains his unyielding severity even in his later abstract works. Leygue introduces some slightly baroque ideas, while Epstein prefers a certain stability.

Giacometti's drawings consist of a thousand strokes and a thousand revisions, and are more concerned with expression than with the indication of volume. They seem at first sight unrelated to sculpture technique, but in fact they do explain the technique of this particular artist who, working in clay, searches for expression in form by way of countless hesitations.

In the same manner as Henry Moore, though without the latter's sombre subject-matter, the engravings and drawings of the Italian sculptor Marino Marini also portray his attitude to reality and his transformations of it. Marini achieves a synthesis of form and movement, though he usually confines himself to filiform style to encompass his volumes. The silhouette of his horses which are tense, and frozen at the moment of elation, are very characteristic of his work. They demonstrate how an apparently hasty sketch can often be in fact a studied work. This very deliberate simplicity reveals a most complete observation of form through the eyes of a sculptor, far beyond the scope of a mere improvized sketch. Manzu also purifies his forms and gives them a vivid realism in his drawings before transforming them into sculpture.

These few examples prove that the draughtsmanship of a sculptor is something particular, very different from that of a painter, and that in spite of the varies forms it may take it never wholly escapes from the three-dimensional technique and conception of its author.

Raymond Cogniat

LIST OF ARTISTS AND ILLUSTRATIONS

ANGRAND CHARLES, 1854-1925 *France*
Maternity 67

BALLA GIACOMO, 1871-1958 *Italy*
Moving Forms 108

BARLACH ERNST, 1870-1938 *Germany*
Kneeling Woman 84

BAZAINE JEAN RENÉ, 1904 *France*
Composition 215

BOCCIONI UMBERTO, 1882-1916 *Italy*
The Water Carriers 113

BON ANGELO DEL, 1898-1952 *Italy*
Landscape 191

BONHOMME LEON, 1870-1924 *France*
Seated Woman with a Hat 111

BONNARD PIERRE, 1867-1947 *France*
Children in the Garden 9
Sunset on the Mediterranean 23

BOURDELLE EMILE ANTOINE, 1861-
1929 *France*
Dancing Girl 157

BRAQUE GEORGES, 1882-1963 *France*
Study for "The Chair" 36
Still Life 203

BRIANCHON MAURICE, 1899 *France*
At the Theatre 164
Woman with Mirror 193

BUFFET BERNARD, 1928 *France*
Head 188

BURCKHARDT CARL, 1878-1923
Switzerland
Male Nude Study 76

CAMPIGLI MASSIMO, 1895 *Italy*
Two Friends 117

CAPOGROSSI GIUSEPPE, 1900 *Italy*
Composition 214

CARLETTI MARIO, 1912 *Italy*
Pure Love 175

CARRA CARLO, 1881-1966 *Italy*
War on the Adriatic 116

CHAGALL MARC, 1887 *Russia, France*
Nude 123
Sketch for "The Fire Bird" 152
Flowers and Fruit 165

CHIRICO GIORGIO DE, 1888 *Italy*
Metaphisical Design 114

CORINTH LOVIS, 1858-1925 *Germany*
Self-Portrait 90

COUTAUD LUCIEN, 1903 *France*
The Prodigal Son 201

CROSS HENRI EDMOND, 1856-1910 *France*
Landscape at Lavandou 22

CZOBEL BÉLA, 1883 *Hungary*
The Road 109
Portrait of Mrs. Ferenczy 172

DERAIN ANDRÉ, 1880-1954 *France*
Two Women 39
The Dancers 41
Almanac (July) 57
Seated Nude 73
Carnaval People 99
Festival 122

DESNOYER FRANÇOIS 1894 *France*
Dressing 187

DESPIAU CHARLES, 1874-1946 *France*
Seated Youth 60
Study for "Apollo" 65

DIGNIMONT ANDRÉ, 1891-1965 *France*
Portrait of a Young Woman 194

DONGEN KEES VAN, 1877 *Holland, France*
Baccarat 40
Head of a Woman 51

DUBUFFET JEAN, 1901 *France*
Portrait of Limbour 186

DUFY JEAN, 1888-1965 *France*
Still Life with Flowers and Glass . . 121

DUFY RAOUL, 1877-1953 *France*
Portrait of Jean Cocteau 64
The Butterfly Ballet 97
The Reception 112
Circus Horses 161

DUNOYER DE SEGONZAC ANDRÉ, 1884
France
Seated Woman 59
Still Life 101

EPSTEIN JACOB, 1880-1959 *U.S.A.*
England
Reclining Nude 169

ERNST MAX, 1891 *Germany, France*
U.S.A.
Composition 133

ESTÈVE MAURICE, 1904 *France*
Composition 258 209

FEININGER LYONEL, 1871-1956 *U.S.A.*
Aquaduct 93

FÉRAT SERGE, 1881 *Russia, France*
Man with Guitar 149
The Circus Clowns 200

FERENCZY BÉNI, 1890 *Hungary*
Portrait of Béla Bartók 130

FOUJITA TSOGOUHARU, 1886 *Japan*
Young Girl Seated 125
Two Asian Heads 129

FRIESZ OTHON, 1879-1949 *France*
Portrait of Fernand Fleuret 17

GEN PAUL, 1895 *France*
14th of July 127

GIACOMETTI ALBERTO, 1901 *Switzerland*
Figure 218

GIMOND MARCEL, 1894-1961 *France*
Head of a Woman 180

GLEIZES ALBERT, 1881-1953 *France*
Maternity 47
Crucifixion 145

GONZALES JULIO, 1876-1942 *Spain*
France
Maternity 156

GRIS JUAN, 1887-1927 *Spain, France*
Man with Glass 31

GROMAIRE MARCEL, 1892 *France*
Nude 141

GRUBER FRANCIS, 1912-1948 *France*
Nude 179

GUTTUSO RENATO, 1912 *Italy*
Sketch for the "Crucifixion" 174
Head of a Woman 196

HARTUNG HANS, 1904 *Germany, France*
Composition 213

HERBIN AUGUSTE, 1882-1960 *France*
Arabesque 138

HODLER FERDINAND, 1853-1918
 Switzerland
  Study for "Enttäuschten"........ 61

HUGO JEAN, 1894 France
  Costume for "Romeo and Juliet" 166

HUMBLOT ROBERT, 1907 France
  Seated Nude 189

JAWLENSKY ALEXEJ DE, 1864-1942
 Russia
  Medusa 88

KANDINSKY WASSILY, 1866-1944
 Russia, France
  Improvisation 32
  Composition 53

KARS GEORGE, 1882-1945 Czechoslovakia
  Nude 66

KIRCHNER ERNST LUDWIG, 1880-1938
 Germany
  Two Couples 83
  Two Women on a Sofa 86

KISLING MOISE, 1891-1953 Russia, France
  Fishing Harbour 100
  Rue de la Gaieté, Paris 162

KLEE PAUL, 1879-1940 Switzerland
  Houses by the Sea 87
  Landscape. The Past 94
  Rose-Coloured Form 104

KOKOSCHKA OSKAR, 1886 Austria
 England
  Reclining Woman 54
  Bouquet of Flowers 181

KOLLWITZ KAETHE, 1867-1945 Germany
 U.S.A.
  Fettered Man 106

KUPKA FRANK, 1871-1957 Czechoslovakia
 France
  Composition 148

LA FRESNAYE ROGER DE, 1885-1925
 France
  Pencil Drawing 14
  Landscape with Nude 30
  Study 37

LAPICQUE CHARLES, 1898 France
  Figure 217

LAUNOIS JEAN CHARLEMAGNE, 1898-1942
 France
  Algerian Girls on the Balcony..... 25

LAURENCIN MARIE, 1885-1956 France
  Portrait of a Young Woman...... 50
  Portrait of a Woman 128

LAURENS HENRI, 1885-1954 France
  Nude 135

LEBASQUE HENRI, 1865-1937 France
  Woman with Red Umbrella 163

LEGER FERNAND, 1881-1955 France
  Composition 137

LEGUEULT RAYMOND, 1898 France
  Interior 182

LHOTE ANDRÉ, 1885-1962 France
  Standing Nude................. 44
  Still Life 139

LILLONI UMBERTO, 1898 Italy
  Luna Hotel, Venice 192

LIPCHITZ JACQUES, 1891 Lithuania
  Figure 53..................... 159

LOUTREUIL MAURICE, 1885-1925 France
  The Guitarist 74

LUCE MAXIMILIEN, 1858-1941 France
  Woman Laundering 29

LURÇAT JEAN, 1892-1966 France
  Sun-Rise 167

MACKE AUGUST, 1887-1914 Germany
  The Yellow Coat 80

MAILLOL ARISTIDE, 1861-1944 France
  Nude Back 34
  Nude Stretched Out 35

MANESSIER ALFRED, 1911 France
  N° 9 in the Prairie 216

MANGUIN HENRI, 1874-1943 France
  Oriental Woman 21
  Tulips 24

MANZU GIACOMO, 1908 Italy
  Head of a Young Woman 131
  Seated Woman Study 154

MARC FRANZ, 1880-1916 Germany
  Two Horses 77
  The Gazel 85

MARCHAND ANDRÉ, 1907 France
  Study of the Sea 206

MARIN JOHN, 1870-1953 U.S.A.
  Circus Elephants 151

MARQUET ALBERT, 1875-1947 France
  Seated Woman 8
  Mirrored Nude 16

MASSON ANDRÉ, 1896 France
  Grass and Flowers 62

MATISSE HENRI, 1896-1954 France
  Still Life 71
  Odalisque 72
  Young Girl at the Window-White
  Dress with Black Belt 146

METZINGER JEAN, 1883-1956 France
  Two Heads 147

MIRO JOAN, 1893 Spain
  People in Movement 95
  Composition 199

MODIGLIANI AMEDEO, 1884-1920 Italy
 France
  Young Woman with Scarf 42
  Portrait of a Man 43
  Study for the "Cariatyd" 49

MONDRIAN PIET, 1872-1944 Netherlands
  Lighthouse Westchapel.......... 52
  Pier and Ocean 136

MOORE HENRY, 1898 England
  Reclining Figure (Study for Sculpture II)....................... 176

MORANDI GIORGIO, 1890-1964 Italy
  Still Life with Glasses and Pitcher 134

MOUALLA SAYGY FIKRET, 1903 Turkey
 France
  The Musicians 98
  Animated Street................ 126

MUELLER OTTO, 1874-1930 Germany
  Two Nudes under the Trees 79

MUNCH EDVARD, 1863-1944 Norway
  Crouching Woman............. 55
  Standing Woman 78

MUSIC ANTONIO, 1909 Italy
  Composition 210

NAY ERNST WILHELM, 1902 Germany
  Composition in Yellow and Red 170
  Composition 171

NOLDE EMIL, 1867-1956 Germany
  Café (After Manet) 89
  Couple Dancing 91

OROZCO JOSÉ CLEMENTE, 1883-1949
 Mexico
  Study 63

OUDOT ROLAND, 1897 France
  Venice 184

PASCIN JULIUS, 1885-1930 Bulgaria
 France
  Two Women 7
  Seated Model 28

PEIRCE WALDO, 1884 U.S.A.
  Nude Bathing 173

PETITJEAN HIPPOLYTE, 1854-1929 France
  Ophélie Bresdin................ 20

PEVSNER ANTOINE, 1886 Russia
  The Accordion Player 107

PICASSO PABLO, 1881 Spain, France
  Mother and Child 11
  Roosters 18
  Family of Acrobats with Monkey 19
  Woman Standing 33
  Standing Nude................. 45
  The Painter and His Model 155
  The Artist and His Model 202

PLANSON ANDRÉ, 1898 France
  Kitchen Interior 103

RATTNER ABRAHAM, 1895 U.S.A.
  Composition 198

RIVERA DIEGO, 1886-1957 Mexico
  Mexican Girl 168

RODIN AUGUSTE, 1840-1917 France
  Nude 10

ROHNER GEORGES, 1913 France
  Study 178

ROUAULT GEORGES, 1871-1958 France
  Girl in Blue 110

SCHMIDT-ROTTLUFF KARL, 1884
 Germany
  Head of a Girl 82

SHAHN BEN, 1898 Russia, U.S.A.
  The Dancers 160

SIGNAC Paul, 1863-1935   *France*
St. Michel Mountain............. 5
Beside the River 12

SINGIER Gustave, 1909 *Belgium, France*
Composition 211

SIRONI Mario, 1885-1961   *Italy*
Study of a Man Taming a Rearing
Horse 119

SLOAN John, 1871-1951   *U.S.A.*
Model Asleep 70

SPAZZAPAN Luigi, 1889-1958   *Italy*
Horse 118

STEINLEN Théophile, 1859-1923
Switzerland, France
Nude with a Handkerchief 26
The Happy Wanderer 102

SZENTIVANYI Lajos, 1909   *Hungary*
Cannes........................ 190

TAL COAT Pierre, 1905   *France*
Large Drawing 207

TERECHKOVITCH Costia, 1902 *Russia*
France
Young Girls on the Beach 183
Young Woman 195

TOUCHAGUES Louis, 1893   *France*
Portrait of Leslie Caron Practicing
(15 years old) 205

UTRILLO Maurice, 1883-1955   *France*
Montmartre: Le Passage Cottin ... 96

VALADON Suzanne, 1867-1938 *France*
After the Bath 27

VALLOTTON Félix, 1865-1925
Switzerland
Child Study 68
Clémenceau 75

VALMIER Georges, 1885-1937 *France*
Still Life with Fish.............. 140

VALTAT Louis, 1869-1952   *France*
The Red Dress................. 38
The Tuileries 124

VIEIRA DA SILVA Maria Helena, 1908
Portugal, France
Abstract Mosaic 204

VILLON Jacques, 1875-1963   *France*
The Three Magi 142
Corneille 143

VLAMINCK Maurice de, 1876-1958
France
Landscape with River........... 56
Landscape 150

VUILLARD Edouard, 1868-1940 *France*
Seated Nude 6

WALCH Charles, 1898-1948 *Germany*
France
Alpine Climber 197

ZADKINE Ossip, 1890   *Russia*
Head of a Man................. 219

CONTENTS

INTRODUCTION

Drawing and Water-Colour as Autonomous Art-Forms 5

Line-Drawing 15

Brush-Drawing 31

MAJOR TRENDS

A General Survey 46

Free Techniques at the End of the Nineteenth and Beginning of the
    Twentieth Centuries:
    The Nabis and the Fauves 48

Expressionism and Jewish Painting 69

New Schools:
    Cubists and Futurists 92

Aspects of Realism.. 115

Poetry and Intelligence:
    Surrealism and Abstract Art 132

SPECIAL TRENDS

The Pleasant Life:
    Women, Fashions, Theatre, Interior Design...................... 153

Technical Uses:
    Advertising, Posters.. 185

Sculptors' Drawings 208

List of Artists and Illustrations.................................. 221